Legislatures

Legislatures

K. C. WHEARE

A Galaxy Book

New York   OXFORD UNIVERSITY PRESS   *1963*

© Oxford University Press 1963

First published as a Galaxy Book, 1963

Printed in the United States of America

PREFACE

THIS book is not a guide to the legislatures of all countries. It confines itself chiefly to countries where the legislature plays some significant part in the system of government, and has done so for a substantial period. Within these limits, moreover, it does not attempt to describe in detail the composition, structure and working of the legislatures concerned. It aims rather at the discussion, on the comparative method, of certain broad themes or issues which arise from a study of the place and purpose of legislatures in modern politics.

I am under a deep debt of gratitude to my friend Professor Peter Campbell of the University of Reading who has read my manuscript with meticulous care, and has made many suggestions for its improvement which I have been delighted to accept. And once again I wish to record how much I owe to my wife's encouragement.

Exeter College, Oxford.   K.C.W.
    24th September, 1962

CONTENTS

Chapter One

MAKING COMPARISONS

I

PARLIAMENTS and congresses and other similar assemblies are commonly called 'legislatures'. The use of the name is convenient and indeed justifiable, but it can mislead. For a large part of the time of these bodies is not devoted to law-making at all. One of their most important functions is to criticize the executive. In some countries they make or unmake governments. They debate great issues of public concern. They constitute 'a grand inquest of the nation'. They act as what John Stuart Mill called 'a committee of grievances', and 'a congress of opinions'.

This variety in the functions of these political institutions is recognized and illustrated by the variety in the names they bear. They are called 'parliaments'— places where talk is carried on, 'talking shops' in the opinion of their critics. They are called 'congresses' or 'assemblies'. They are composed of houses of representatives, houses of the people, houses of assembly, houses of commons, chambers of deputies, and senates. There is nothing in these names which suggests that their functions are even concerned with the making of laws, much less confined to it. And even in the United States, where the name 'legislature' is commonly used, the national legislature is called 'Congress', and only twenty-six out of the fifty states speak officially of the 'legislature', nineteen use the term 'General

Assembly',[1] three 'Legislative Assembly,'[2] and two 'General Court'.[3] All describe their upper houses as 'Senates', and the use of 'House of Representatives' to describe the lower houses is almost invariable.

What we call 'legislatures', then, concern themselves with many important functions other than the making of laws. Moreover, even where law-making is concerned, they are not usually alone in the field. In the first place, they do not necessarily make all the laws. It is common for powers to make laws to be conferred upon the executive or the president, the monarch, ministers, or officials. Sometimes these law-making powers are conferred upon the executive by the constitution—they are original legislative powers. An example is the Constitution of the Fifth French Republic, which describes the matters upon which the parliament may make laws and leaves the rest to regulation by the executive. Sometimes these law-making powers are conferred upon the executive by the legislature—they are delegated legislative powers. The nature and extent of these powers of executive rule-making vary from country to country. The point of importance is that in most countries what we call the legislature does not do all the legislating.

In the second place, even when the legislature itself is engaged in the process of law-making, it is common to find that it is not authorized to complete this

[1] Arkansas, Colorado, Connecticut, Delaware, Georgia, Illinois, Indiana, Iowa, Kentucky, Maryland, Missouri, North Carolina, Ohio, Pennsylvania, Rhode Island, South Carolina, Tennessee, Vermont, and Virginia.

[2] Montana, North Dakota, and Oregon.

[3] Massachusetts and New Hampshire.

process without the assent of the executive. Sometimes this is no more than a formality, as in the United Kingdom, where the assent of the Queen is necessary before a Bill can become law, and where that assent is not refused. Or it may be a reality, as in the United States, where the President is empowered to veto a Bill passed by the Congress, and where the President's veto can be overriden only by a two-thirds majority in each of the two houses of Congress. In all the American states, except North Carolina, the governor may veto measures passed by the legislature, and his veto cannot be overruled, in most cases, except by a two-thirds majority in each house. These veto powers are by no means a dead letter in the United States; they are exercised frequently and effectively. Legislatures thus cannot expect invariably to legislate alone.

Yet, when all this has been said, it remains justifiable to speak of parliaments and congresses and the like as legislatures. And the justification, shortly stated, is that these bodies are, if not actually, at least potentially superior to other law-making bodies. Where the executive has some original legislative power, it is common to find that its ordinances can be amended or overriden by the assembly. Where the executive exercises delegated legislative power, the parliament may withdraw the delegation and may override any exercise of the power delegated. Where the executive's assent is needed to complete the process of legislation, that assent, where it is not a formality, may, if the assembly is sufficiently united and determined, be dispensed with. The last word about what the law is to be rests with the assembly.

What is more, many of the other important functions

of a parliament or congress are connected with and arise from its function of law-making. The discussion of grievances and the criticism of the executive and the debating of great or small issues are naturally and necessarily linked with the process of making or amending the law. In particular it is proper that a representative assembly should seek redress of grievances before passing a law to authorize the spending of money by the executive or the raising of taxes upon the citizens. The occasion of law-making provides the opportunities for that debate and discussion and criticism which occupy so large a part of the time of many assemblies.

For reasons of this kind, it seems proper to speak of these institutions as legislatures. But, in the chapters that follow, while we shall describe the part which legislatures play in the making of laws, we shall devote more space still to the analysis and appraisal of the other important functions which legislatures perform.

2

Legislatures differ strikingly in size. At one extreme there are houses so large that, like the British House of Commons of 630, the French National Assembly of 482, the Italian Chamber of Deputies of 596, the Indian House of the People of 500, the German Bundestag of 499, or the American House of Representatives of 437, they seem like a mass meeting. At the other extreme there are houses so small that, like the Senates of Nevada or Delaware with 17 members, they seem like a committee. Some are surprisingly large— the House of Representatives of New Hampshire has 400 members for a population of about 600,000. New

York State, on the other hand, with a population of about 17 million is content with an assembly of 150 members. It may seem surprising also that the United States and India should have houses which are considerably smaller than those of Britain, Italy, or France, in spite of the fact that they seek to represent populations many times larger. It is true that the American and the Indian people are represented not only in their national legislatures, but in the legislatures of their constituent states. Even so, it is permissible to wonder whether it is the British, Italian and French houses that are remarkably large or the American and Indian houses that are remarkably small.

In general, the legislative houses—particularly the lower houses—of most national sovereign states range in size from 100 to 300 members. The Canadian House of Commons, for example, has 265 members, the Belgian lower house 212, the Swedish lower house 232, the Finnish house (it has one only) 200, the Swiss lower house 196, the Netherlands lower house 150, the Danish house (it also has one only) 179, the South African House of Assembly 160, the Irish lower house (Dail) 144, the Norwegian Storting 150, and the Australian House of Representatives 124. Among lower houses of less than 100 members may be mentioned the New Zealand House of Representatives of 80, and the Icelandic lower house of 40. Here again, if we are to get the picture in true proportion, we must remember that in some of these countries, the people are represented, as in the United States, in state or provincial councils as well. Canadians are represented in the legislatures of their ten provinces, Australians in the parliaments of their six states, the Swiss in the legislatures of their twenty-two cantons, and the South Africans in their five provincial councils.

3

The size of a legislature has some interesting and important effects upon its organization and operation. A very large assembly produces problems of accommodation. If all the members are to be provided with seats a large chamber will be needed. That this can be done must be admitted, for most countries with large legislatures have done it. Britain, however, is an exception, and as it attaches importance and significance to being an exception, something must be said about it. The British House of Commons has decided deliberately that the Chamber in which it meets shall be too small to provide each of its 630 members with a seat.

The old chamber of the House of Commons, which was destroyed by bombing in the Second World War, could accommodate 346 members. It is true that there was room in the galleries for another 100, and on a crowded day members sat there. But that was a very different thing from having a seat on the floor of the Chamber itself, though it is said that at least one enterprising member (Mr. Pemberton Billing) asked a question in the House from the galleries. When the time came to consider plans for rebuilding the chamber, some members suggested that it might be so constructed that there could be room on its benches for all the members. This proposal strikes one, at first sight at any rate, not only as humane, but as inevitable, if not obvious. If a man is elected to sit in the legislature, ought he not to have somewhere to sit? But the

House of Commons rejected the proposal and the present chamber still fails by a long way to accommodate all the members. There can surely be no legislative chamber in any other country (which believes in parliamentary institutions) constructed deliberately on this principle.

How could it possibly be justified? A great House of Commons man said this:

'The characteristic of a Chamber formed on the lines of the House of Commons is that it should not be big enough to contain all its members at once without overcrowding, and that there should be no question of every member having a separate seat reserved for him. The reason for this has long been a puzzle to uninstructed outsiders, and has frequently excited the curiosity and even the criticism of new members.'

These are the words of Mr. Winston Churchill, speaking as Prime Minister in the House of Commons (then sitting in the Chamber of the House of Lords) on 28 October 1943, and commending the proposal to build the new chamber of the House of Commons on the same lines as the old. And he gave these reasons for his view:

'If the House is big enough to contain all its members nine-tenths of its debates will be conducted in the depressing atmosphere of an almost empty or half-empty chamber. The essence of good House of Commons speaking is the conversational style, the facility for quick informal interruptions and interchanges. . . . But the conversational style requires a fairly small space and there should be on great occasions a sense of crowd and urgency. There should be a sense of the importance of much that is said, and a sense that great matters are being decided, there and then, by the House.'

This sounds, and no doubt is, something of an orator's attitude to the House of Commons. But the House agreed with Mr. Churchill and there is no doubt that in these words he expressed part of the British view of the purpose of a legislature. It exists to be a grand forum of debate, a sounding board for governments, an audience to be called together in a crowd on great occasions and to disperse when the excitement is over.

Let us look a little further into this question of the relation between size and seating arrangements in the British House of Commons. Suppose it were decided to give each member his own individual reserved seat, what consequences would follow? Immediately you would come into conflict with a strongly held British belief not only about whether there should be seats for all, but also about how such seats as there are should be arranged.

Seats in the British House of Commons are arranged in rows facing each other across the chamber, and separated by a gangway running the whole length of the Chamber, with the Speaker's chair at one end. To the right of the Speaker sit the supporters of the government; to his left those who oppose it. But if everyone is to have a seat, and if you have an equal number of seats on each side of the Chamber, the supporters of the government, being in the majority, are bound to overflow on to the opposition side. Is this a bad thing? After all, on a crowded day, government supporters seek accommodation on the opposition side and occupy it if they can find it. That, admittedly, is temporary. But to have one's allotted seat permanently reserved on the opposition side and to have to speak from that side in support of the government apparently does violence to the feelings of many members of the House of Commons. Indeed, in the course of the debate in 1943 one member, Mr. Rhys Davies, said: 'I prefer meeting my political opponent face to face. I do not like turning at a slant to argue with him.'

To an 'uninstructed outsider' such delicacy might seem strange. And all the more so when he discovers that in the Canadian House of Commons, which has a chamber similar in shape and in the arrangement of seats to the British chamber, no such inhibitions apparently prevail. Each and every member has his own allotted seat, with the result that supporters of the government do sit on the same side as the opposition if the size of the government's majority requires it.

And what is the alternative? To provide more seats to the Speaker's right than to his left would produce a curiously shaped chamber. To be on the safe side it would be necessary to allow over 600 seats on the Speaker's right to provide for the eventuality of a government with a very large majority. On the speaker's left 300 seats at least would be needed for an opposition which came near to the government in numbers. Here is a larger chamber than ever. What is to be done? How can the idea of the government and opposition facing each other across the chamber be combined with the idea of seats for all? Are they irreconcilable

The fact is, that in an assembly of any size, it cannot be done, without producing too large a chamber. In a small assembly there is less difficulty. There can be enough accommodation for a very large body of government supporters or for a very large opposition within a chamber of moderate size. The only way out, for a large legislature, is a compromise, and it is a compromise which the British House of Commons rejected in 1943. It is the semicircular chamber or amphitheatre. By this means the supporters of the government can be seated on the right of the Speaker and the opponents of the government on his left, but it is true that at a certain point somewhere past half-way round the semicircle, government and opposition supporters are sitting side by side. This is, in fact, the method of seating adopted in the parliament of Australia at Canberra, and it is found also in the chambers of some other legislatures in the Common-wealth. They have diverged from the model of West-minster in this matter. Outside the Commonwealth it is almost invariably adopted. It is the usual system in European legislatures. It is found in the chambers of the Senate and the House of Representatives in Wash-ington, and most of the legislatures of the fifty con-stituent states of the United States. Why could not the House of Commons adopt it in 1943?

Here again the answer can be given in Mr. Church-ill's words. Speaking in the same debate on 28 October 1943, he said:

'Its shape should be oblong and not semicircular. Here is a very potent factor in our political life. The semi-circular assembly, which appeals to political theorists, enables every individual or every group to move round the centre, adopting various shades of pink according as the weather changes. I am a convinced supporter of the party system in preference to the group system. . . .

The party system is much favoured by the oblong form of chamber. It is easy for an individual to move through those insensible gradations from Left to Right, but the act of crossing the floor is one which requires serious consideration. I am well informed on this matter, for I have accomplished that difficult process, not only once but twice. Logic is a poor guide compared with custom. Logic, which has created in so many countries semi-circular assemblies which have buildings which give to every member not only a seat to sit in, but often a desk to write at, with a lid to bang, has proved fatal to parliamentary government as we know it here in its home, and in the land of its birth.'

Though Mr. Churchill named no country, all his hearers knew which he meant. It was of France that they thought when they heard his words. And it is true that France has a semicircular chamber. The French have a large assembly—even if it is not now quite so large as the British House of Commons—and they seat them in an amphitheatre, ranged from left to right not only physically, but also politically, with the Communists on the extreme left of the presiding officer, the most conservative group on his right, and other groups in the centre. There they sit, graded and shaded. The language of politics owes part of its vocabulary to the seating arrangements of a semicircular chamber—left, centre, left of centre, right of centre, right and extreme right. And it is interesting to notice, in passing, that it was France which gave these terms to politics. In the French National Assembly of 1789, the nobles as a body took the position of honour on the President's right, and the Third Estate sat on his left. The significance of these positions, which was at first merely ceremonial, soon became political. And it is in the modern French chamber that the arrangement of groups from left to right physically corresponds closely with the shade of their opinions politically.

The justification of the seating arrangements in the British House of Commons, then, is this. The members of the House cannot all have seats, for that would be practicable only in a semicircular chamber. A semi-circular chamber would undermine the two-party system. You must be either for the government or against it; you must be on one side of the chamber or on the other. An oblong chamber not only assists you, but compels you to take sides. 'We shape our build-ings', said Mr. Churchill, 'and afterwards our buildings shape us.'

It may be suggested that this argument is a little far-fetched. The oblong chamber may be a good sym-bol of the British two-party system, but we can hardly say that it causes it or is an essential pre-requisite of it, or even that it has a principal share in maintaining it. Can it be seriously suggested that if some Conser-vative and Labour members of parliament actually sit next to each other continuously, they will find it easier or tempting to change places? Is there much evidence that government and opposition members in the Australian parliament are encouraged by the semi-circular arrangement of seats to change their allegi-ance? Not at all. The fact is that the essence of the British system lies not in the oblong chamber nor in the inadequate seating accommodation for members, but in the ranging of two sides behind their leaders, one forming the government and the other the opposi-tion. The supporters of each side sit together, with the bulk of the government supporters on the Speaker's right and the bulk of the opposition on his left. This system can operate in a semicircular chamber no less effectively than in an oblong chamber—perhaps in some ways more effectively, for the semicircular chamber has the advantage that it makes it possible to accommodate a large assembly in a more convenient space, a space in which not only all can sit, but all can hear.

It is interesting to notice that the lower house of the legislature of the West German Republic (the Bundestag) decided in 1960 to convert its arrangement of seats into an arrangement on the model of a rough horseshoe or semicircle. This change had long been advocated by the president of the Bundestag who felt that the existing arrangement was too much like a lecture room and that the opposing parties should confront each other in debate. Not all members supported the proposal, and it was natural that the leader of the small Free Democratic Party should argue that the change to an arrangement on the new model presupposed a two-party system which did not exist in Germany. Whether in fact the new arrangement would have affected the German political system remains to be seen for the change has been postponed on financial grounds.

4

Clearly one must resist the temptation to become too fanciful about the significance of seating arrangements and of the shape of the chambers in legislatures. At the same time it is not too misleading to say that, when one looks at the way in which different legislatures deal with these matters, at least three distinct, though not exclusive, notions of the purpose of a legislature are illustrated.

The first is that the purpose of a legislature is to divide itself up clearly into those that are for the government and those that are against it. In the legislatures of Britain and of the other members of the Commonwealth this notion is usually clearly illustrated and symbolized. Whether they give each and all of the members a seat or not, and whether they seat them in an oblong chamber or in a semicircular chamber, they organize themselves on the principle that members are either for the government or against it. Those for the government will all sit together on one side of the presiding officer and those against it will all sit together on the other side, and each side will, to a substantial extent at any rate, confront the other. And it would appear that it is this principle of organization which has attracted the interest and support of those who advocated the rearrangement of seating accommodation in the German Bundestag.

Then there is a second notion, which is illustrated in the arrangements for seating in most of the European legislatures and which is found also in the national and state legislatures of the United States. This is the notion that the purpose of a legislature is to reflect and exhibit the party composition of the representatives of the people or of the country. The chamber of the French National Assembly constitutes the prototype of this system. But although this can be done most neatly in a semicircular chamber, it is not impossible in an oblong chamber as the practice of the legislature of the Netherlands can demonstrate. If one visits the chambers of the two houses of the States-General in Holland, one is struck with their resemblance to the British House of Commons—they are rectangular in shape, with benches arranged in rows on each side and facing each other across the chamber. But members sit in party groups to the left and right of the presiding officer, roughly in accordance with their political complexion as expressed in the language of 'left' and 'right'.

But party composition and structure need not be exhibited with the complete logic of left to right. In Denmark, for example, the legislature is accommodated in a semicircular chamber, and the members sit together in party groups, but they occupy positions agreed among the groups themselves. They sit from left to right physically, but not necessarily politically. In American legislatures members of the same party sit together, but their position to the left or right of the chair is governed by tradition. In the House of Representatives and in the Senate at Washington, for example, Democrats, by custom, sit to the right of the presiding officer and Republicans to the left, regardless of which party is in the majority, but as the chambers are semicircular inevitably at some point some Democrats and Republicans find themselves sitting side by side.

In these arrangements of seats, then, although the members of a party or group all sit together, their place in the chamber is not governed by whether they are for the government or against or whether they are in the majority or in the minority. As a result there is no alignment of parties in the chamber by which the supporters of the government confront the opposition.

In a third arrangement of seats, the emphasis on party alignment and party solidarity is given less prominence. Sweden and Norway give illustrations of this system. Sweden adopts a semicircular arrangement of seats, but it ignores party affiliations altogether in the allocation of seats. Members are seated by constituencies. And as in Sweden members are elected by proportional representation in multi-member constituencies, a further refinement is introduced. In the Swedish upper house members are seated within their constituency group according to the order in which they were declared elected at the last general election; in the lower house, members are seated within their constituency group according to the number of sessions they have previously attended. Norway also arranges its members in constituency groups in its semicircular chambers, with the constituencies arranged in alphabetical order.

To someone brought up under the British form of parliamentary government and equally to those familiar with the French system, this must seem an odd arrangement. To have the government's supporters and its opponents all mixed up instead of being gathered together to confront each other across the chamber; or to have members of a party who are supposed to be working together scattered about the chamber instead of sitting in a compact group—this seems a startling idea. Yet it is a system strongly maintained by the Swedish and Norwegian legislatures. An attempt to change the system in Sweden about forty years ago, and to have members sitting in party groups was not supported and has never been revived. It is not too fanciful to suggest that by this system of seating

Sweden and Norway recognize and symbolize the notion that members of a legislature are not merely party supporters, but are also representatives of their own district and that they have this common interest and duty irrespective of their party affiliations.

5

These differences in the way in which the functions of a legislature are regarded are illustrated also by the different arrangements made in legislative chambers for the seating of members of the government. In the legislatures of the United States and those established on their model the significant thing about seating arrangements for the executive is that there are none. Not only are members of the executive disqualified from membership of the legislature but, save for exceptional visits from the President of the United States or a state Governor, and for the fact that the Vice-President of the United States or the Lieutenant-Governor of a state presides over the upper house of the legislature, members of the executive do not appear in the legislative chambers. When the President or a Governor appears to deliver a message in person, he speaks usually from the clerk's desk, in front of and a little below the seat of the presiding officer.

In countries where ministers are permitted to appear and speak in the legislative chamber (whether they are members of it or not) some interesting difference in seating arrangements are found. Members of the government have an allotted place, but the differences arise in the relation of this place to the place where their suporters are to be found. In Britain and in most other members of the Commonwealth and in countries like South Africa and the Republic of Ireland which retain the British type of parliamentary system although no longer members of the Commonwealth, the government is allotted the front benches on the right of the Speaker (on the left in Ireland) with its supporters behind and flanking it. The leaders of the opposition are allotted the front bench on the opposite side with *their* supporters behind and flanking them. This arrangement is maintained whether or not the members are seated in a semicircle or in rows facing each other. Members take up their places in the chamber, therefore, according to whether they support the government or are opposed to it, and they change sides with their changing fortunes.

Where members are seated without regard to whether or not they support the government, it must follow that if the ministers are allotted a fixed position in the chamber, it can seldom happen—and then only by accident—that they are seated with their supporters. Thus in the French National Assembly under the Fourth Republic (and in the Chamber of Deputies under the Third) the two lowest rows of seats in the centre of the semicircle were reserved for ministers. Governments which had the support of groups in and around the centre, therefore, would have their supporters behind them, though they would have their opponents to the right and left of them. There were many occasions, however, when those sitting behind a French Cabinet were not or were not all its supporters. In the lower house of the parliament in the Netherlands a bench is reserved for the government opposite the presidential dais. No members sit behind this bench and the government is therefore cut off from its supporters. In Sweden and Norway where members are seated by constituencies, irrespective of party affiliation, it is clear that wherever the government sits, it will be unlikely to find its supporters concentrated behind it. In Sweden, for example, in the lower house the government sits in the front rows on the right of the presiding officer. By accident their supporters might be behind them and flanking them, but it would be an uncommon accident.

These arrangements for seating the government illustrate the three broad views of the function of a legislature. Where the legislature is thought of as composed primarily of supporters and opponents of the government, then members take their seats on the government side of the chamber or on the opposite side according to their views. Where the government sits determines where members sit. Where a chamber is principally thought of as exhibiting the party composition of the legislature, then the seating of the government need have no relation to the seating of members and vice versa. It can be determined by convenience and tradition. And this will apply all the more in a legislature where members are seated by constituencies, as in Sweden and Norway. More will be said of the relation between government and legislature in succeeding chapters. It is mentioned at this stage to illustrate the way in which, by differences in seating arrangements, there are often symbolized in the chambers of a legislature, differences in the political and constitutional systems of a country.

6

There is one piece of furniture commonly found in the chambers of European legislatures which is usually regarded with distrust, if not derision, by admirers of the British House of Commons. This is the rostrum or tribune. 'Harangues from a rostrum', said Mr. Churchill in this same debate in 1943, 'would be a bad substitute for the conversational style in which so much of our business is done.' The rostrum is an accepted feature of continental chambers. The presiding officer sits upon a raised dais or platform, and below him or in front of him or to one side is a reading desk or pulpit from which all members speak. This is undoubtedly a more formal way of doing business than is usual in the legislatures of the Commonwealth or of the United States. In these legislatures members speak from their places. The use of the rostrum, one would think, encourages orations, and set speeches; it makes informal intervention difficult, if not positively disorderly. In a way, too, it can make the task of the presiding officer in keeping order more difficult, for he finds himself more or less in the firing line of any hostile or disorderly remarks which may be flung at the orator from the body of the chamber. It is much easier for a member speaking from his place to resume his seat when the presiding officer rises to give a ruling or call him to order than it is for a member who is speaking from a rostrum. It is easier, also, for a presiding officer to order a member to resume his seat, if he is speaking from it, than if he is speaking from a rostrum and is required to go back to his place in the chamber itself. When the rostrum is used, orators appear in fact, if not always in form, to be addressing the house and not the presiding officer, in contrast with the practice of Commonwealth and American legislatures where all remarks must be addressed to the chair. The proceedings can become an engagement between orator and assembly, with the presiding officer somewhat excluded from the arena and at a disadvantage in his attempt to keep control of the proceedings.

So, at least, it appears to those brought up under the Commonwealth or American systems. That there is some substance in these opinions seems certain, though they may be exaggerated. It is reasonable to assert, at any rate, that the use of the rostrum and the type of discussion it evokes is a distinctive mark of the European way of doing business, and not only in legislatures, but in conferences and committees of all kinds. The practice of addressing the chair from the place where you sit is similarly characteristic of the method of doing business in Anglo-Saxon countries.

But, while 'harangues from a rostrum', as Mr. Churchill called them, are not a feature of business in the British House of Commons or in the legislatures of Commonwealth countries, harangues from a dispatch box are, as no one knew better than Mr. Churchill. Here is an important and significant exception or qualification to the general statement that in Britain and other Commonwealth countries members of the legislature speak from where they sit. For the leaders of the government and of the opposition advance from the front benches upon which they sit and speak from a dispatch box on the table of the house. Though this is not a rostrum, it is a strategically well placed pulpit from which to make an harangue. But notice that it is reserved for front benchers only.

This is an illustration of the pre-eminence given in Britain and other Commonwealth countries to the 'front-bencher', to the leaders of the two sides in the great forum of debate. Whereas in European legislatures any member, be he leader or follower, minister or private member, front bencher or back bencher, has access to the rostrum, in the legislatures of the Commonwealth all but the leaders on the front bench speak, as it were, from the audience, from the body of the hall. This arrangement symbolizes the different attitude not only towards the government, but also towards leadership generally in these legislatures from that found in European assemblies, a difference which will be explained more fully in later chapters.

One further illustration may be offered. In the Australian House of Representatives in Canberra, a seat has been placed on each side of the table of the House, one on the Speaker's right for the Prime Minister or whoever is in charge of the government's business at the moment, and one on the Speaker's left for the leader of the opposition or his equivalent. They sit opposite each other, obviously marked out as the leader of their team, and they talk across the table informally from time to time as the debate continues. This arrangement would seem a startling innovation in the British House of Commons, but the principle it symbolizes is accepted there.

7

Legislatures differ strikingly in the status and functions of their presiding officers. Their position may be said to range from the extremes of the Speaker of the British House of Commons with his complete impartiality and detachment from party to that of the Speaker of the American House of Representatives who is the leader of the majority party in the House. The nature of these extremes must not be exaggerated. In his function as a presiding officer the American Speaker is expected to act impartially and by custom usually votes only if there is a tie. Apart from this, however, he enters fully into party politics. In Britain, though the Speaker once in office is detached from party, it is usual when there is a vacancy in the office, for the majority party to fill it from one of its own members. Once elected, however, a Speaker who is willing to be re-elected in succeeding parliaments, will be re-elected although his former party may now be in a minority. This was illustrated in 1945 when the House of Commons, with the Labour party holding a large majority, re-elected Colonel Clifton Brown to the Speakership, although he had been a Conservative and was first elected Speaker in 1944 when the House had a Conservative majority. He was re-elected in the new House of 1950 when Labour still held a majority, though a very small one. He retired from the House at the General Election of 1951. That election produced a Conservative majority and the new Speaker, Mr. W. S. Morrison, was a Conservative. He was re-elected in the new House, still with a Conservative majority, which was returned at the General Election of 1955. He retired at the General Election of 1959 and his successor, Sir Harry Hylton Foster, a Conservative, was elected by the new House which, once more, contained a Conservative majority. (It will be seen that, by the operation of these practices, Labour, though providing a majority in the House of Commons from 1945–51, has not yet had the opportunity to provide a Speaker.)

To ensure or assist the impartiality of the Speaker in Britain certain practices and usages are followed or commended, but it cannot be said that they are so completely formulated or accepted by all concerned as to rank as binding rules. It is usual, for example, to select the Speaker from the back benches, from those who do not hold or have not held office in the government. Yet Speaker Morrison had been Minister of Agriculture from 1936 to 1939 and had held other ministerial offices until 1945, though he had not held office in the interval until his election to the Speakership in 1951. Speaker Hylton Foster had been Solicitor-General in the parliament of 1955–9, but on the other hand this office is itself somewhat detached from party politics. Again it is thought to be desirable that the election of the Speaker should be unanimous; that he should have the support of all parties. Yet in 1951, when Speaker Morrison was first elected, a candidate from the Labour side was nominated in opposition. The choice of Speaker Hylton Foster in 1959 was criticized by the Labour Party. There is apparently no complete agreement yet about the rules which should be accepted in making the choice of a Speaker.

An attempt is made, also, to protect the Speaker's impartiality by seeking to ensure that he is not opposed in his constituency at a general election. But it is not always possible to ensure this, even if the official party organizations are willing—and they have not always been willing. In the General Election of 1895 Speaker

Gully, a Liberal, was opposed in his constituency by a Conservative. In the next ten general elections the Speaker was returned unopposed. But in the General Election of 1935 Speaker Fitzroy, a Conservative, was opposed by an official Labour candidate, and Speaker Clifton Brown was similarly opposed in 1945. In 1950 however, when all parties had agreed not to oppose Speaker Brown, his election unopposed was prevented by an independent candidate who, though defeated, polled a considerable number of votes. Again in 1955 Speaker Morrison was opposed by an independent Socialist, although the Labour Party officially did not nominate a candidate. Thus although it would seem that the parties are coming to agree that the Speaker should be returned unopposed, it is not possible to prevent the free enterprise of the electors from producing a candidate in opposition to him. And there is no disposition yet in Britain to adopt the practice of the Republic of Ireland where, since 1927, by law the Speaker, if willing to accept office again in the new house, is declared re-elected in his constituency without having to go to the polls. The idea has been proposed in Britain but rejected on the ground that it results in the disfranchisement of the electors in the Speaker's constituency—yet this is in fact what would happen if the objective of the official party policies in not putting forward candidates in opposition to the Speaker were achieved. In Ireland, however, it may be argued that this result is not so rigorously applied, for Irish constituencies are multi-member constituencies, not single member constituencies as in Britain, and there is room for party contests in the Speaker's constituency in the filling of the remaining seats.

Although there have been examples recently of the choice of a Speaker in Britain who has held office in the government, it seems well established that a Speaker once elected, will regard himself as no longer a candidate for any office in the government in future. When he retires as Speaker, he retires from the House of Commons and, although he is offered a seat in the House of Lords—and usually accepts it—he has retired from party politics. His impartiality in office is assisted, therefore, by the knowledge that he hopes and seeks for nothing at the hands of the government of the day, whether it be of his party or not.

It has been thought desirable to go a little into detail about the standing of the Speaker of the British House of Commons because, generally speaking, the presiding officers of the chambers, upper and lower, in the other countries of the Commonwealth, and what is more, in the legislatures of continental Europe come much nearer to the position of the British Speaker than to the Speaker of the House of Representatives in Washington. Their function is to be presiding officers, not party leaders. But the extent to which they seek or are able to achieve the impartiality and detachment of the British Speaker varies a great deal from country to country and from time to time. Though they are certainly not party leaders, they are often party men; they may have given up party politics for the time being, but they may not have given them up for ever. They may have held office in the past and they may hope to hold it again in the future. They may have achieved the Speakership as a consolation prize but they may not be content with it. They may desire to be impartial and to keep out of party conflict, but the assembly may not allow them to do so. Much depends on the traditions and code of behaviour of the members. If a Speaker's rulings are questioned, if he is heckled and interrupted, if members indulge frequently in uproar and interjections, if baiting the Speaker is regarded as all part of the game, then inevitably he finds himself involved in party conflict. His authority depends in the end upon the support and respect he receives from the house, and it is upon this that the strength of the Speaker of the British House of Commons and the relative weakness of presiding officers in other assemblies ultimately depends.

In this matter, too, the size of the assembly has an effect. In a small house a government's majority may be numbered in two's or threes, and the Speaker's casting vote may determine from time to time whether the government is to stay in office or not. There have been a number of examples in Commonwealth legislatures where the government holds office solely on the Speaker's casting vote, and it has been accepted that he has been elected as Speaker from among the government's supporters on the understanding that he will keep the government in office. In such situations it cannot be expected that the Speaker will be allowed to detach himself from party politics, even if he wishes to do so. In a large assembly like the British House of Commons, on the other hand, the likelihood of the government's holding office by the Speaker's vote is more remote. What is more, in a large house it is not unusual to find a small group of members who find their interest in questions of parliamentary procedure and who are attracted to a career in the tasks of chairmanship. To them the Speakership and other presiding offices, such as the chairmanship of committees of the House, seem a worthy goal of parliamentary ambition, instead of or in preference to the holding of office in the government. The British Speakership has many times been filled by such a person.

The states of the American union follow the practice, very largely, of the Congress at Washington. The Speakers of the lower houses of the state legislatures combine, as does the Speaker of the House of Representatives at Washington, the dual role of presiding officer and party leader. The majority of the upper houses also follow the practice of the Senate at Washington. By the Constitution of the United States, the Vice-President of the United States presides over the Senate. This strikes one as odd at first sight. It would seem essential that a chamber should have the right to choose its own presiding officer and that it would choose one of its own members. The Vice-President is chosen by the electorate and he is not a member of the Senate. Similarly in the majority of the states, the Lieutenant-Governor, similarly chosen by the electorate, presides over the state senate, though not a member of it. (Odder still, in Nebraska where there is only one chamber, the Lieutenant-Governor presides over it.) In the absence of the Vice-President or of the Lieutenant-Governor, the Senates choose their own president *pro tempore*, and if the Vice-President succeeds to the Presidency (as has happened seven times up to 1962) or the Lieutenant-Governor to the Governorship, the President *pro tempore* acts as president continuously. This practice of having a presiding officer not elected by the assembly itself and not being a member of it, may be compared with the position in

the British House of Lords where the Speaker is the
Lord Chancellor, not elected by the House, but
appointed by the government; but, in this case, though
the Lord Chancellor need not be a peer, he is invariably created one.

To lump together the presiding officers of different
legislatures in this way is inevitably unsatisfactory, for
their position varies tremendously and subtly and
indeed is seldom static. Some of their important functions will be mentioned in later chapters. At this stage
it seemed essential, however, to stress differences, to
emphasize that these differences arise from differences
of history, political and constitutional ideas, tradition
and social customs which determine the way in which
an office, which at first sight might seem likely to be
much the same everywhere, will work in a given community. And this is true as much of the office of presiding officer in the legislatures of Commonwealth
countries which are said to be based on the 'model'
of Westminster as of the presiding officers of continental
European legislatures.

8

A word on one final matter—the method of voting
adopted in legislatures. Here some interesting differences arise. Almost all legislatures permit a decision on
relatively uncontroversial matters by a voice vote. The
presiding officer asks those in favour to say 'Aye' and
those against to say 'No' and judges from the volume
of the replies which side has won. But if members wish
to proceed to a formal vote then a variety of methods
is found. And it is interesting to find that in this matter
also the size of an assembly and its seating arrangements

have an influence upon what is or can be done. If each member has his own allotted seat, it is possible to take a vote by asking members in favour of a motion to rise in their places, and thereafter those opposed to it to rise and a clerk can check the results. This is one of the methods of voting used in the Congress of the United States, in the French National Assembly, and in the two houses of the legislatures of Sweden and the Netherlands. It is possible also, by this method, and particularly in an assembly of small size to obtain a list of the names of all the members voting and how they voted, for the seats they occupy are known and their attendance in their allotted places can be checked off on a seating plan.

There could, however, be room for dispute by a member about whether or not he had been counted on the right side and for this and other reasons when it is desired that there should be a record of how members voted, recourse is usually had to the roll call. This can be very lengthy. It has been known to take up to an hour in the French National Assembly. When used in the American House of Representatives it frequently takes half an hour or more, for the names of the 435 representatives are called and thereafter the names of those who did not respond on the first call are called again. It is used in the parliament of the Netherlands, also, but of recent years the method of voting by standing has become more widely used than heretofore.

In order to save time and yet obtain a record of how members voted, various electrical voting devices have been adopted. They have been installed in the legislative chambers of Sweden and Finland (for example) and of thirty states in America. Each member by pressing the appropriate button at his desk signifies his vote; and this is recorded on a screen or lighted panel so that the member himself can see that his vote is correctly recorded: and the machine calculates the result. People with a repugnance to mechanical devices enlarge upon the possibilities of fraud, break down, mistake and practical joking which these machines open up. Yet legislatures which have adopted them show no desire to give them up. It was calculated by Mr. George B. Galloway, an American expert on Congress, that the installation of electrical voting equipment in the House of Representatives of the United States would save one month each session.

To the outsider, at first sight at any rate, the method of taking a division in the British House of Commons must seem very odd. And not to outsiders only. Mr. David Lloyd George, Prime Minister from 1916 to 1922, described it as 'barbarous' in 1930 when he gave evidence to a select committee of the House which was considering how parliamentary time might be saved, 'Uncomfortable and inconvenient', he added. The method—and it is the only method of taking a division permitted by the House—is for members to pass into the lobbies that run down each side of the chamber, one for the government supporters on the Speaker's right and one for opposition supporters on his left. There they are counted by tellers—there are two in each lobby, each pair consisting of one appointed from the 'ayes' and one from the 'noes'—and their names recorded by clerks. It takes from ten to fifteen minutes to register a division, the result of which in most cases, is a foregone conclusion. Major Milner (later Lord Milner of Leeds), a very experienced Labour member of the House of Commons, and particularly well versed in the procedure of the House of which he was Deputy Speaker has described the system as 'quite unjustifiable.' He was giving evidence in 1944 to the select committee that was considering the rebuilding of the Chamber. He admitted the difficulty of devising a satisfactory alternative for a House of so large a membership and where members did not have their own allotted seats. But he was revolutionary enough to mention electrical systems of voting. But Mr. Baldwin, another former Prime Minister had different views. He said to the select committee of 1930 that 'a walk through the lobbies restored the House to a sense of perspective'. Members 'came back much cooler and much quieter'. There is, indeed, no move to change the system. But it is seldom adopted in the legislatures of the Commonwealth overseas where divisions are taken by roll-call or by members being counted as they sit in their allotted seats.

So, in what might seem the simplest of all matters, the mere mechanics of counting votes, legislatures differ, and, what is more, believe firmly that their differences matter.

Chapter Two

MAKING THE LEGISLATURE

I

ALMOST all the legislatures with which we are concerned are chosen by some form of election. Even the British House of Lords, the overwhelming majority of whose members hold their seats by hereditary succession, or by appointment to an hereditary or to a life peerage, has a small elected element—there are sixteen representative peers of Scotland, elected for the life of a parliament, by the hereditary peers of Scotland from their own number. The Senate of Canada, on the other hand, has no elected element; all its 102 members are appointed by the Governor-General on the advice of the Prime Minister of the day. Occasionally, too, a predominantly elected house has a small non-elected element. The Indian House of the People, for example, contains two members nominated by the President of India to represent the minority community of Anglo-Indians, which might otherwise not be represented. Generally speaking, however, legislatures are made by election. There is, indeed, great variety in the methods by which these elections are organized and carried out. To describe them in detail in this chapter would be impossible, even if profitable. What it is important to understand is the nature and significance of these different methods, for they help to explain the differences in the status and functions of the legislatures themselves from country to country. The best way in which to appreciate these variations, perhaps, is to try to answer in general terms a series of broad questions about the making of legislatures.

2

Let us ask first: Who decides when elections are to be held? A short answer to this question is that in some countries the decision lies, in a considerable degree, within the discretion of the executive, and that in others, it does not. Britain provides a good example of the former class and the United States of the latter. In both countries the maximum term of the legislature is fixed by law, but whereas in Britain the executive— that is to say the Queen, acting on the advice of a Prime Minister—can dissolve the legislature before the expiry of its full term and call for elections to a new House of Commons, in the United States no such power rests with the President. What is true of Britain is true also of the lower houses in other countries of the Commonwealth, in South Africa and in Ireland. A similar power is lodged in the executive in some European countries, though it is not always exercisable entirely at the discretion of the executive. The monarch may dissolve the lower houses of Belgium, Holland and Sweden at any time; the King of Denmark and the President of Finland can dissolve their single chamber legislatures at any time. In France under the Third, Fourth and Fifth Republics a power of dissolution has always been lodged with the President, but there has been much difference of opinion about the circumstances in which it should be exercised. Under the Third Republic the President could dissolve the Chamber of Deputies with the advice and consent of the Senate. Thus, though the power to dissolve was placed in the hands of the head of the State, its exercise was not controlled by the government, but by one house of the legislature which was empowered to call for the dissolution of its partner. The power was exercised once only, in 1877, and was thereafter regarded as almost, if not entirely, a dead letter. In the Fourth Republic it was provided in the Constitution that the lower house (now called the National Assembly) might not be dissolved at all in the first eighteen months of its life. Thereafter if, within a period of eighteen months, two governments fell after the refusal of a vote of confidence or on the passing of a vote of censure, the President could dissolve the assembly on the advice of the cabinet. As votes of confidence and of censure were governed by special rules and as it was possible to cause the resignation of governments without resort to these special devices, the assembly was able to avoid a situation in which it might bring dissolution upon itself. In fact this situation arose only once, when the assembly was dissolved in 1955. In the Fifth Republic the President may dissolve the assembly, (he did so in 1962), though he is required, before so doing, to consult beforehand the Prime Minister and the Presidents of the Assembly and the Senate. He may not, however, dissolve the Assembly again within a year of his previous dissolution, nor may he dissolve it while he is exercising his special emergency powers.

In Italy the power of dissolution of the Chamber of Deputies is in the hands of the President (though he may not dissolve it in his last six months of office), but he is required to exercise his power only after consultation with the president of the chamber. In Norway the Storting may not be dissolved at any time before its full four year term has expired. And it is interesting to note that even in Sweden, where dissolution by the executive is permitted, the term of the newly-elected house runs only for the unexpired portion of the four-year term of its predecessor, so that, irrespective of dissolutions, general elections occur in Sweden every four years—in each leap year in fact.

What has been said so far refers to the dissolution of the lower houses of a legislature. Some upper houses may not be dissolved at all. Chambers not recruited by election, such as the House of Lords and the Canadian Senate obviously cannot be dissolved. The same is true of the French Senate although it is indirectly elected. Some upper houses, like the Australian Senate, can be dissolved only to resolve a deadlock between them and the lower house in circumstances laid down by law. But in Belgium, Holland and Sweden the upper houses may be dissolved by the head of the state on the advice of the government, in the same way as the lower houses. In Italy the President of the republic may dissolve the upper house after consulting the president of that house. In Ireland it is provided that a general election to the upper house always takes place automatically within ninety days of the dissolution of the lower house.

There are in some states provisions that amendments of the constitution cannot be completed until an election of one or both houses of the legislature has occurred and the proposed amendment has been subsequently approved by the newly-elected houses. In Belgium an election of both houses is required; in Sweden an election of the lower house: in Denmark and Norway an election of the single chambered legislature. Elections of this kind, though formally decreed by the head of the state, do not really fall within the category of elections whose time is determined by the executive. They are the consequence of the provisions of the law of the constitution and may be said to follow automatically from the decisions of the legislatures themselves to initiate the process of constitutional amendment.

It is one thing for the executive to have the power to dissolve the legislature more or less at its discretion; it is quite another for it to exercise this power. There is considerable variation from country to country in the use made of the power. In Britain, in other Commonwealth countries, and in South Africa and Ireland, it is accepted practice for the executive to use the power to dissolve the legislature before the expiry of its allotted term if to do so might be thought desirable for electoral advantage, for the resolution of a political crisis or for the endorsement or rejection of some questions of political policy. There is much room for disagreement about the circumstances in which dissolution is proper or justifiable, but the fact is that the power *is* used by the executive. In European countries, however, the power is much more sparingly exercised. It has been noted already that in the years from 1875, under the Third and Fourth French Republics, dissolution was resorted to only twice. There has been no dissolution in Sweden since 1921. It may well be that the position in Sweden is affected by the provision that a chamber elected after a dissolution continues only for the remainder of the normal four-year term.

In European countries it is clear that the dissolution

is regarded as a weapon to be used sparingly and then chiefly to resolve a political crisis such as a dispute between the executive and the legislature which cannot be otherwise dealt with. The two dissolutions of the lower house in Holland in this century—in 1933 and 1958—fall into this category. What we do not find in European states is the use of the dissolution by the government of the day to fix the appropriate time, in terms of electoral advantage, at which to hold the election, a practice which is regarded as normal in Britain, in other Commonwealth countries, in Ireland and in South Africa. European legislatures are expected to run their full term and resort to dissolution is thought to be justified only as a last resource available to assist in the resolution of a political crisis. Any attempt by the executive to bring the legislature before the electorate before the expiration of its fixed term in the absence of a crisis would be resented by the legislature, regarded with suspicion by the electorate and would perhaps do the executive harm, not good. These differences in attitude to the use of the power of dissolution by the executive are a symbol of the differences in the relationship of the legislature to the executive in European states and in the countries of the Commonwealth, of which more will be said in a later chapter.

One restriction upon the power of the executive to decide when elections to the legislature are to be held must be mentioned and emphasized for it is important. Although the executive may shorten the life of the legislature by dissolution, it cannot extend its life and thus postpone elections to a more convenient time. In most states the term of a legislature is fixed in the constitution and can be extended only by a constitutional amendment. Where, as in the United Kingdom, it is fixed by act of parliament (the Parliament Act of 1911, which fixed the term at a maximum of five years) it can be extended only by an amending act, as was done for example in the Second World War when the parliament elected in 1935 and due to expire in 1940 was prolonged for a year at a time, by act of parliament, until 1945. In cases of this kind it is the legislature itself not the executive, which decides to postpone the date of the election.

Moreover, although the executive can and does choose the occasion for dissolving the legislature in countries such as Britain, certain other important matters connected with the election are regulated either by act of the legislature or in the constitution itself. Such matters as the interval that must elapse after the announcement of the election before the election itself is actually held, and the date by which candidates must be nominated are laid down by law and the scope left to the executive to manipulate these dates to its own advantage is considerably curtailed.

In countries, like the United States and Switzerland, where the executive has no power to dissolve the legislature, the term of the legislature is fixed by the constitution while the date of elections is fixed either by the constitution or by act of the legislature itself or, more usually, by a combination of both. Thus in the United States, the term of the House of Representatives in Washington is fixed by the Constitution at two years, while that of a senator is six years, with a third retiring every two years. For elections to the Senate and House of Representatives the Constitution provides that 'the times, places, and manner of holding elections for senators and representatives shall be prescribed in each state by the legislature thereof; but the Congress may at any time by law make or alter such regulations. . . .' In 1872 the Congress fixed as election day for federal offices the Tuesday after the first Monday of November in even-numbered years. The result is that, in all states except Maine, whose constitution prescribes elections in September, the date fixed by Congress is adopted, both for the election of the Congress of the United States and also for the election of state legislatures.

In a country like the United States, therefore, the dates of elections are known well ahead of time. The executive has no power to alter or affect them. The legislatures themselves have little discretion about them either. They are a fixed and indeed rigid element in American politics of considerable importance in governing the manœuvres of legislators.

3

A second question is: Who may elect the legislature? The answer is that universal adult suffrage is now the common franchise for lower houses of the legislature. By adult is meant being over the age of 21 and it includes females as well as males. Adult suffrage in this sense prevails in Britain and in most countries of the Commonwealth, in Ireland, and in most of the countries of Western Europe. There are occasional exceptions. In South Africa the right to vote for the legislature of the Republic is confined to Europeans. Women lack the right to vote for the national assembly (the lower house) in Switzerland, a surprising fact in the light of the country's reputation as a model democracy. In Holland, again, the minimum age for a voter is 23, not 21. In the United States the age of 21 is chosen for federal and state elections save in Georgia where the age is 18.

In addition to the requirement of a minimum age, most countries naturally prescribe that voters must be citizens, and if not citizens by birth, must have been citizens for a prescribed period of years. Residence within a constituency for a prescribed period and registration upon an electoral roll by a prescribed date are also required—an obvious necessity if voters are to be organized into constituencies and reliable electoral rolls prepared. But there are few survivals of the property qualifications which were common requirements for the franchise in the nineteenth century and in the earlier decades of the twentieth. Some states in the United States enforce a literacy test, but the constitution of the United States forbids the passing of laws which would discriminate in voting qualifications between people on grounds of race, colour, previous condition of servitude, or sex.

Where the upper houses of legislatures are concerned it is sometimes found that the minimum age limit for voters is higher than for the lower house. Thus the minimum age for an elector for the upper house in Holland and in Italy is 25, as against 23 for the lower house in Holland and 21 in Italy. But these differences are becoming rare. In Sweden, for example, the voting age for the upper house, set at 27 in 1921, was reduced to 23 in 1937 and to 21 in 1941.

There are some generally recognized disqualifications

upon the right to vote. Persons of unsound mind, persons serving prison sentences, undischarged bankrupts, and those convicted of offences against the electoral laws, particularly in relation to corrupt practices, are among the classes excluded from the franchise in many countries. There are, of course, exceptions and additions to these classes. Peers may not vote in Britain; bankrupts may vote in Sweden; persons convicted of drunkenness twice within a given period lose the vote in Holland.

Who may be elected? is the third question we may ask. Not all those entitled to elect are, as a general rule, entitled to be elected. The field is sometimes narrowed by requirements stricter than those prescribed for the voter. Take citizenship, for example. In the United States every voter must be a citizen, but to be a member of the House of Representatives at Washington, a person must have been at least seven years a citizen, and to be a Senator, he must have been at least nine years a citizen—the Constitution of the United States itself lays this down.

Generally speaking, the minimum age requirement for membership of the legislature is higher than that for an elector. Though an elector need be no more than 21 in the United States, for example, a member of the House of Representatives must be at least 25, and a Senator at least 30. Many state constitutions also prescribe a higher age for state senators than for electors, though there are few which require members of the lower house to be more than 21. In European legislatures higher age qualifications for legislators than for electors are commonly found. In the Netherlands the minimum age for membership of either house of the

legislature is 30. In Belgium a member of the Chamber
of Representatives must be at least 25, and a Senator
at least 40; in France a member of the National
Assembly must be at least 23 and a Senator at least 35;
in Italy a member of the Chamber of Deputies must
be at least 25 and a Senator at least 40; and in Sweden
the ages are 23 and 35 respectively. In Britain, however, and in the Republic of Ireland and in most
countries of the Commonwealth there are no requirements of this kind. The minimum age for membership
of the legislature is the same as that for qualification as
an elector.

Requirements about residence provide some interesting and important differences between countries.
It is almost inevitable that residence should be required as a qualification for an elector. It is upon this
basis that a system of constituencies can be organized,
that electoral rolls can be drawn up and that voters can
be checked to secure, among other things, that they do
not exercise more votes than they are entitled to. But
should candidates for election have to satisfy a similar
requirement? Here the American system differs from
that in many other countries. The Constitution of the
United States requires that a Congressman must, when
elected, be an inhabitant of that state in which he shall
be chosen, and the same also is required of a Senator.
Custom, moreover, requires that a member of the
House of Representatives reside in the district he
represents—though there have been exceptions to
this rule. This 'locality rule' as it is called has a
great importance in the United States and may
be considered at once a cause and a reflection of
the strong local attachments of American legislators,

especially members of the House of Representatives. They regard themselves as elected to look after their district and their future political prospects are as a rule inevitably confined in practice to that district.

Some other countries have a residence requirement. In Sweden, for example, candidates for the lower chamber must reside in the district for which they stand; no such restriction is imposed upon candidates for the upper house, though in practice, in the last thirty years, a great and increasing proportion of members of the upper house do so reside. By contrast, in the United Kingdom, and in most countries of the Commonwealth, there is no residence requirement imposed by law. It is true that many candidates, especially for rural constituencies, may be local residents. It is true also that many candidates, when elected, become residents in their constituencies at least for some of the time. But there is no requirement of law or custom which prevents non-residents from being candidates in a particular district, or from moving from district to district in search of a seat, or a sitting member from seeking a new constituency at a subsequent election. The 'carpet-bagger' is a familiar figure in British elections in all parties.

A common disqualification for membership of a legislature is employment in the government service. The Constitution of the United States puts the rule succinctly: 'No person holding any office under the United States shall be a member of either House during his continuance in office.' Thus the separation of legislature from executive is secured. A similar rule applies in all the states of the Union. And the exclusion from the legislature is not confined to members of the executive—it extends also to all judicial officers. Even in countries where the separation of powers does not apply so completely as in the United States, where, as in Britain and the Commonwealth countries and in some of the democracies of Western Europe, a system of parliamentary cabinet government prevails and the heads of the executive are permitted or required to sit in the legislature, the exclusion applies to all other office holders almost invariably.

But there are some interesting and curious exceptions. No one is excluded from the legislature in Sweden by virtue of the holding of office. Public servants are still found in the two houses, though high officials are less common as members than they used to be. In the Netherlands where even ministers are not permitted to be members of the legislature, civil servants are not disqualified. If elected to the house they cease to perform their official duties, but they are not required to vacate their office. They may return to it in due course.

The rule in Britain is applied in one curious way. Members of the House of Commons do not resign their seats. If they wish to cease to be members during the life of a parliament they apply for appointment to certain nominal, sinecure offices under the Crown— usually the Stewardship of the Chiltern Hundreds and the Stewardship of the Manor of Northstead—and upon appointment thereby vacate their seats.

In Britain, too, there are certain other disqualifications not commonly found elsewhere. Peers may not sit in the House of Commons, a disqualification which has removed more than one able member of the House from the active pursuit of the highest political offices upon succeeding to a peerage. The case of Mr. Anthony Wedgwood Benn in 1961 who was required to vacate his seat in the House of Commons on succeeding his father as Viscount Stansgate drew attention to this rule. Clergy of the Church of England, of the Church of Scotland, and of the Roman Catholic Church may not sit in the House of Commons—a disqualification which does not apply to the ministers of other denominations. The Swiss Constitution restricts membership of the National Council to lay men.

4

How are candidates for election chosen? This is our fourth question. Under party government it is understood that there will be official candidates of the parties presenting themselves for election. But there will have been usually some competition among people to be the official candidates of the party. There is great variety in the methods adopted to choose official candidates. Without going into detail, it is worth mentioning here one or two features of this system of selection.

In countries where legislatures are elected by territorial constituencies, the choice of candidates is usually made by the constituency organization of the party, subject, as a rule, to some degree of approval or influence from the central party organization which, in most cases, is providing some of the funds for the campaign. In Britain, where the locality rule does not obtain, the central office of a party will have some suggestions to offer about suitable candidates and may press them strongly upon the local organization. The selection locally is made by a committee and ratified by a local meeting of party members. These matters are left entirely to the parties themselves and are not regulated by the state.

It is in the United States that steps have been taken to regulate these selections by law through the various systems of primary elections. In primary elections voters choose the candidates of the party who will be put forward at the later election to the legislature. In parts of the country where one party—such as the Democratic Party in the southern states—has a strong hold, selection in the primary almost invariably ensures election. The primaries are, in fact, the real elections. Two types of primary deserve mention. There is the 'closed' primary—used in most of the states—in which each voter may take part in the election of the party of which he is a member. There is the 'open' primary— used, for example, in Wisconsin, Michigan, Minnesota, Montana, and Utah—in which all voters may participate, each voter selecting in the polling booth the candidates of his choice, thus avoiding a prior declaration of his party allegiance.

The object of instituting and regulating primary elections was to associate the people with the process of choosing party candidates and thus to curb the power of party oligarchies and bosses. Clearly, on the system of selection which operates in countries like Britain, a very small group of people is associated with the process. But it is by no means clear that opening the process to the public through the system of primaries has appreciably weakened party oligarchies in the United States. The voters can be organized with considerable success to ratify the principal choices of the party leadership.

5

Are members of the legislature elected directly or
indirectly? is our fifth question. The short answer to
this question is that the lower houses of legislatures are,
almost invariably, directly elected, while it is common
to find indirect election used for upper houses, particularly in the legislatures of Western Europe. Thus
the French Senate is chosen by electoral colleges in
each department, consisting of the members of the
lower house for that department, together with the
members of the departmental councils and representatives of the communal councils of the department. The
Swedish upper house is elected by members of provincial councils and of certain municipal councils. The
upper house of the Netherlands is similarly chosen.
In Belgium the majority of the members of the upper
house are directly elected, but there is a proportion
(46 out of 175) indirectly elected by provincial bodies.

In the United States direct election for senates is
the invariable rule. The choice of the Senate of the
United States was indirect, by state legislatures, from
the inception of the Constitution until, in 1913, the
17th Amendment of the Constitution was proclaimed
by which direct election was instituted. In all state
senates, the rule is now direct election.

In the constitutions of Commonwealth countries
practice varies. The Senate of Australia is elected
directly by the people of the states, as in the United
States. The upper houses of the state legislatures are all
directly elected, except that of New South Wales,
where indirect election by the members of the lower
house prevails. The Indian upper house, the Council

of States is, save for twelve nominated members, indirectly elected by the members of the legislatures of the several states.

Generally speaking, indirect election plays a subordinate part in the making of legislatures. Upper houses are usually subordinate to the lower houses. In many cases they are intended to provide for some sort of provincial or regional representation and thus indirect election by local assemblies is an appropriate method of recruiting them. But it is important to remember that in some societies, as in some African states, where tribal or other traditional authorities are strong, indirect election from bodies of this kind is probably the most effective method of making national legislatures. Territorial constituencies with direct election would, in many such cases, be an artificial, not to say unintelligible method of organizing the electorate.

6

What electoral systems are adopted in the making of legislatures? In attempting to answer this sixth question, we encounter a most technical topic. It will be necessary to treat it without going into detail. Broadly speaking, countries are divided into those which use some system of proportional representation (and there are many such systems) and those which do not. Britain and the United States are among the principal countries which reject proportional representation. They adopt what may be accurately called the first-past-the-post system. They use single-member districts and the candidate who gets the highest number of votes is declared the winner. In other words, what is required to be elected is not an absolute majority (i.e.

more votes than all the others put together) but a plurality.

It is well known that this system produces inaccurate results. Even when only two parties are involved the proportion of seats gained by a party in the legislature may be greater or less than the proportion of votes cast for it in the country. Where there are more than two parties it can happen that the candidate elected is not desired by a majority of the voters. Thus a Labour candidate in Britain who receives a plurality over a Conservative and a Liberal candidate is unlikely to be the choice—even the second choice—of the majority of the voters. In spite of these admitted defects, however, the system has persisted.

Schemes to make electoral systems more accurate have been frequently put forward and are in operation in many countries. There are, first, the systems which attempt to deal with the kind of situation just described where a candidate is elected on a plurality. One of these systems is the Second Ballot. If no candidate receives an absolute majority at the first election, a second is held, say a week later. In some examples of this method the second ballot is confined to the two candidates who secured the greatest number of votes in the first ballot; in others, three or more of the top candidates are permitted to run again; and sometimes there is no restriction at all.

The Second Ballot was used during most of the life of the Third French Republic. It was operated in single member constituencies from 1875–85, 1889–1919, and 1928–40, and in multi-member constituencies from 1873–5 and 1885–9. If at the first ballot candidates did not obtain an absolute majority of votes cast, and a number of votes at least equal to one-quarter of the registered electors in the constituency, a second ballot was held, at which all candidates at the first election could run again if they chose, as well as candidates who had not run at the first election. At the second ballot an ordinary majority or plurality sufficed. Although the system was abandoned under the Fourth Republic, it was revived again, with single member constituencies under the Fifth and used in the elections of 1958. The law required, however, that a candidate might stand for the second ballot only if he had stood for the first and had obtained at least 5 per cent. of the votes.

A method resembling the Second Ballot is the Alternative Vote. This is used in single or multi-member constituencies and is like casting a provisional second ballot at the same time as the first. Electors indicate their preferences among the candidates by placing the figures, 1, 2, 3, 4, 5, etc., beside their names. If no candidate has an absolute majority, the candidate with the lowest number of first preferences is eliminated and his second preferences are then distributed among the other candidates. If this does not give any candidate an absolute majority, then the next lowest candidate is eliminated and his second preferences are distributed and so on until a candidate obtains an absolute majority. This is the system used with single member constituencies in electing the Australian House of Representatives, and the lower houses of the state legislatures in Victoria, New South Wales, South Australia and Western Australia.

It is pointed out, however, that such methods as the Second Ballot and the Alternative Vote have the weakness that they give the elector an opportunity of obtaining the second best (which may not always seem to him to be better than nothing at all) but they do not help him to get the candidate or the party he prefers most. And they do not meet the objection, inherent particularly in all single member constituency systems that by, for example, 'wasting' the votes cast for unsuccessful candidates the result in terms of seats in the legislature may distort or falsify the result in terms of votes cast in the country. To meet these objections systems of proportional representation have been devised and are used in most of the countries of Western Europe.

One such system—the use of the Single Transferable Vote—has operated in the Republic of Ireland (formerly the Irish Free State) almost since its establishment in 1922. It requires (like all systems of proportional representation) multi-member constituencies instead of single member constituencies. Electors mark their ballot papers in order of preference, 1, 2, 3, etc. The number of valid votes cast is divided by the number of seats to be filled, plus one, and this figure, plus one, gives the 'quota'. On the first count, any candidate who reaches this quota is declared elected. Then any surplus of votes above the quota which have been cast for him or them are taken and distributed according to the second preferences marked on them, so that these votes will not be wasted. If no candidate has secured the quota, the bottom candidate is eliminated and his second preferences distributed. And so the process goes on, distributing surpluses or eliminating candidates until the requisite number of candidates obtains the quota. The process of counting is extremely lengthy and the rules about the proper distribution of surpluses extremely complicated. The Single Transferable Vote has been used in elections to the Tasmanian House of Assembly since 1907, to the Australian Senate since 1949 (replacing the alternative vote in multi-member constituencies) the South African Senate since 1909 and the legislature of Manitoba.

In the parliamentary countries of Western Europe, however, the Single Transferable Vote has not been adopted. Instead some forms of what is generally called the 'List' system of proportional representation have been tried. Multi-member constituencies are used, and there is a requisite quota to qualify a candidate for election. In the simplest form of the list system, electors are confronted with a series of party lists for one of which they may vote, and seats are allocated to the party in accordance with the quota. Candidates are elected in the order in which they have been placed by the party organization upon its list. This method was used for elections to the Reichstag in Germany from 1919–33 and with slight modifications in the elections to the legislature of France in 1945 and 1946.

But there are many variations. In some countries electors are allowed to choose between voting for a party list as a whole or voting for one or more candidates on a party's list. This is the kind of system which operates in Belgium, Sweden, Denmark, Norway, and the Netherlands. In Switzerland still greater freedom is allowed. Voters for the lower house, the National Council, are allowed to distribute their votes freely among the various lists. This is known as *panachage*. Each elector has as many votes as there are seats to be filled. The number of votes cast for candidates in each list is first added up and seats are allocated to the parties in proportion to the totals. Then the seats are filled up from the candidates within the party list in the order of the total votes they have received. By this method control over the order in which candidates are elected is removed from the party organization.

One problem about voting by the list system is what to do with the surplus of votes left over after seats have been filled in accordance with the quota. There are various devices for dealing with this. One is to allow parties to ally themselves together for this purpose. The unused votes of the parties are pooled together to make up a quota to elect one or more candidates from the parties in the alliance which have done rather better. This is called *apparentement*, and it also is permitted in Switzerland. It was adopted as part of the electoral law in Italy in 1953 and in the elections of 1951 and 1956 in the Fourth French Republic. Or there is the method used in the Weimar Republic of Germany by which unused votes were totalled together for the whole country and made up quotas from which additional party members could be elected from provincial or national party lists. And there may be mentioned, finally, the system used in the Federal German Republic since 1946, whereby a proportion of members is elected by the first-past-the-post system as in Britain or the United States, and the remainder are chosen from party lists in proportions which ensure that the representation of the parties in the legislature corresponds to the total of votes cast for them in the country as a whole. And perhaps the logical conclusion is reached in Israel where the whole country is treated as one electorate, voting is by a rigid party list system and seats are allocated in the legislature to candidates from the lists in the order determined by the party organization in accordance with the number of votes cast for the respective lists.

A discussion about the merits of different electoral systems comes down in the end to the question of what it is that elections to a legislature are for. If their purpose is first and before all else to give effect with the greatest possible accuracy to the opinions of the electors about who should sit in the legislature, then some system of proportional representation has to be adopted. There is a great deal of room for argument about which system is the most accurate. There is room for argument, too, about whether it is the electors' opinions about parties only which you wish to measure accurately, or whether they are to be encouraged to express their views also about individuals. Variations of proportional representation to accommodate both these points of view have been invented or operated, as we have seen.

For this accuracy of representation, assuming that it can be achieved, a price must be paid. Proportional representation means multi-member constituencies. It does not commend itself, therefore, to those who think that there is value in the single member constituency because of its smaller size, and the direct link between the elected member and his electors. The list system, again, puts a great deal of power in the hands of central or provincial party organizations who compile the lists. The elector finds himself asked to choose between lists of candidates, of none or few of whom he has heard. Selection of candidates by local bodies is replaced by choice by remote party managers. Proportional representation does greater justice to minor parties, but this in turn can produce a situation where no single party has a clear and workable majority. Simple plurality systems, though crude and misleading, tend to produce legislatures with a clear, if distorted, answer. And they discourage the creation and growth of more than two parties. Again, electors who prefer a single ballot paper which demands no more of them than to place a cross against the name of the candidate they prefer, and who like to understand how the result of an election is calculated—however unpalatable the result may be—will prefer the first-past-the-post system to schemes of proportional representation.

Then by-elections are difficult, if not impossible, under proportional representation. It is true that if a seat falls vacant, an election to fill it can be held in the constituency, but it will be an election in a multi-member constituency to fill a single seat and it cannot be conducted strictly in accordance with proportional representation. In most countries where proportional representation exists, vacancies are filled up either by substitutes elected for this specific purpose at the time of the general election, or by the unsuccessful candidate next on the party list or in some such way. In some countries, however, by-elections are a lively part of the political system and are regarded as valuable guides to public opinion or valuable opportunities for party conflict. To do without them would be to remove an important political institution. This view is held in Britain and in Commonwealth countries, for example, and is regarded as one more argument against proportional representation.

The supporters of proportional representation would

be most unlikely to agree with what has been stated in the last paragraphs. They could point out that in Britain under the simple plurality system the elections of 1923 and 1929 produced a House of Commons in which three parties had a substantial number of seats and that as a result a minority Labour Government took office. And the election of 1950 produced a House of Commons in which the Labour Party's majority was so small and so clearly unworkable that another election had to be held in 1951. The British system, therefore, cannot be relied upon invariably to produce that clear and unmistakable answer in a contest between two parties which is claimed as one of its advantages over proportional representation. There is evidence, also, from the experiences of countries which have used proportional representation that this system does not always or even usually produce unstable governments, while it is noted that France, where cabinet instability was notorious under the Third and Fourth Republics, did not in fact use proportional representation for the greater part of that time.

Many factors influence the choice of an electoral system in a country. Prejudice, tradition and an inability to understand or listen to the explanations of electoral experts are among them. But not least important, of course, are the interests of the existing parties, particularly in so far as these interests are represented in the legislature. In most states the electoral system, even if it is prescribed in the constitution of the state, cannot be altered except with the consent of the legislature. In some states, such as Britain and France, most Commonwealth countries and the United States, the legislature is free to decide whether the country shall have proportional representation or not. It is surely too much to expect that a legislature would alter the system of election by which it was itself chosen, unless the party or parties holding a majority in the legislature thought they would gain, or at any rate, not lose by so doing. It is not surprising that the Liberal party in Britain advocates proportional representation and that the Conservative and Labour parties regard the plurality system as, with all its imperfections, workable. Mr. de Valera became dissatisfied with the results which proportional representation gave in Ireland, and after the General Election of 1957, although his party was returned to office, he obtained the passage of a Bill through the legislature to abolish the system. It was defeated, however, in 1958 by a narrow majority in a referendum of the electors. In France the electoral system has been frequently changed in an attempt to assist the fortunes of parties in the legislature or to prevent other parties from gaining seats, and almost every general election has been preceded by a campaign to revise the system in existence at the time. It was altered for the General Election of 1958 and had been altered, to fit the political circumstances of the moment, before four of the preceding ten elections. France is an extreme case, but it must be accepted that in all countries the effects on party fortunes and the political consequences to the existing legislature, are bound to have an important, if not a decisive, effect in determining what a country's electoral system is and whether or not it will be changed.

7

There is one matter which has a very close connexion with fairness and accuracy of representation and which is even more important than the method of voting and that is the delimitation of electoral districts. It is necessary to ask, therefore, as a seventh question, How are electoral districts determined? In some countries the constitution lays down certain principles to govern the delimitation of districts; in others the matter rests entirely in the discretion of the legislature; in some both constitution and the law of the legislature determine the matter; in some it is left to the executive; in some it is the task of an independent commission.

At first sight it would seem obvious that the fairest division would be that of constituencies as near as possible of equal numbers of electors. But this is not generally accepted, for it could mean, for one thing, that urban areas obtained a greater number of seats in the legislature than rural areas. Some rural constituencies, also, might be very large, too large, it could be argued, for one or even three members to look after. Rural interests would feel that they could be neglected in the legislature, that industrial and manufacturing interests would have too large a say in determining policy. Though rural areas might be small in population, their contribution to the national income and in particular to the country's exports might be very much greater than that of the urban areas. In the framing of tariff policy, in the planning of economic development and in the provision of social services their interests might easily be subordinated to those of the urban population. For reasons of this kind it is sometimes decided—and in some cases embodied in a country's constitution—that rural areas should be given a greater representation in the legislature than their populations warrant and this is justified as fairer representation though not accurate representation.

Where the power to determine the demarcation of electoral districts rests with a legislature, the temptation to use it for party advantage is very great. This may lead to a demarcation remaining unaltered, in spite of population movements and changes; or to new areas being drawn in defiance of equality of numbers so that safe or safer seats can be created for a particular party or parties. The abolition of seats, which a new demarcation can involve, is naturally viewed with disfavour if it removes a seat safe for the party in power, and with impartiality if it removes a seat safe for the opposition. Operations designed to re-draw the lines of constituencies to favour a party's electoral interests are called 'gerrymandering'.[1] There are few countries in which it does not occur in a small measure at any rate.

In an attempt to reduce it to the smallest possible extent constitutions and laws require a redistribution

[1] The word 'gerrymander' was invented in 1812 when Elbridge Gerry was Governor of Massachusetts. The legislature of the state, in which the Democrats had a majority, re-drew the boundaries of the electoral districts of the State Senate so as to favour the candidates of the Democratic Party. A map of one such district, of a very strange shape, hung on the wall of the office of a newspaper editor named Russell. An artist, remarking on the odd shape of the district, added a head, wings and claws to it and said: 'That will do for a salamander!' 'Gerrymander!' said Russell, and the new word was invented. There is a picture of the district, as improved upon by the artist, in J. Winsor, *Memorial History of Boston*, Vol. 3, p. 212.

of seats at regular intervals upon principles of equality or of agreed weightage. But legislatures are slow to act upon these provisions. Great inequalities between districts are found in many American state legislatures; in some rural districts are predominant and have remained so in spite of considerable population changes. Legislators and parties do not work to abolish the seats they occupy and plans for 'redistricting', as it is called, come to nothing. Nor must it be assumed that to provide districts of roughly equal size is a guarantee that gerrymandering has not occurred or is not possible. Lines can be so drawn that the appropriate number of a party's supporters to win the seat are on the right side of the line and an appropriate number on the other side to win the adjoining seat also. A careful redistribution of supporters can produce a successful gerrymander while equality of electoral districts is still maintained as a principle. Even the lines drawn by an impartial commission can be scrutinized and judged by the parties from this point of view.

In Britain the redistribution of seats is now carried out at intervals of not less than ten nor more than fifteen years; it is based upon the proposals of independent commissions; but changes require the approval of both the House of Commons and the House of Lords. It is not free from party controversy, but charges of gerrymandering are not now seriously put forward. In most Commonwealth countries the task is confided to impartial electoral commissions, but a 'weightage' is often conceded to the less populous areas in the law which directs the commission on how to carry out its task. The task itself is much more complicated than appears at first sight. To draw lines on a map so that areas contain roughly the same number of people is relatively simple, but in fact considerations of geography, communications, community of interest, tradition and the like must all be taken into account. And the whole matter is intensely political—a fact which even an impartial commission cannot be expected to rule out of its consideration entirely.

8

A final question is: Who decides when a legislature, once elected, shall be called together to do its business? This is an important question. A first step towards the destruction of democracy is usually a refusal to call the legislature together or a dismissal of it if it is already sitting. To guard against this possibility, the constitutions of many countries provide that the legislature must be called together annually or at some fixed interval, and in some cases even prescribe the date upon which it must convene. Thus the constitution of the United States provides that Congress shall assemble at least once in every year and such meeting shall begin at noon on 3 January unless the Congress shall by law appoint a different day. The legislature alone, therefore, can decide when it meets. The constitutions of the various states in the United States contain similar provisions. The constitution of the Fifth French Republic provides that the parliament will meet in two ordinary sessions a year, the first to begin on the first Tuesday of October and to finish on the third Friday of December; the second to open on the last Tuesday of April and to last not longer than three months. The legislature meets thus by constitutional right; it does not depend upon the will of the executive.

This principle of independence is usually found in continental legislatures. In Belgium, Holland, Denmark, Norway, and Sweden, for example, the chambers meet on dates fixed in their constitutional law—in Belgium on the second Tuesday of November, in Holland on the third Tuesday in September, in Denmark on the first Tuesday in October, and in Norway and Sweden on 10 January, unless it is a Sunday, when it meets on 11 January.

In most Commonwealth countries, however, although the constitution provides for an annual meeting of the legislature, it is left to the discretion of the government to decide the date of the meeting. In practice, however, well established rules or understandings make it certain that the legislature meets at regular times and the approximate dates of the opening of sessions can be predicted. In Britain no law requires the annual meeting of parliament and in form, therefore, it is within the discretion of the Queen, on the advice of the government, to call it or not to call it as she pleases. But as laws must be passed and money spent and collected, the strongest of inducements exist to require the executive to call parliament together. Its new session begins each year about mid-November. At the same time, this difference of procedure in Britain and most Commonwealth countries on the one hand, from that of the United States and of European countries in the power of the executive to call the legislature into session is one more illustration of the difference in status and mutual relation of executive and legislature in these two groups of countries. Of these differences and their significance more will be said in Chapter Four.

Chapter Three

INFLUENCING THE LEGISLATURE

I

LEGISLATORS, once chosen, are seldom left for long to their own devices. We would misunderstand profoundly the working of legislatures if we thought of them as bodies which, between elections, thought things out in isolated tranquillity, independent, free to initiate or to decide matters as they thought fit, influenced only by members' contact with each other. Legislatures are in fact constantly under pressure from persons and institutions outside themselves, and what they do is influenced greatly by these pressures. Elections are indeed but one of the ways and occasions of influencing legislatures, and they are not necessarily the most important. To understand the life of a legislature in between elections, it is necessary to know of some of the forms in which influence is exerted on a legislature.

Legislators may begin life in a newly-elected parliament under the influence of pledges which have been given to the electors either by themselves individually or by their party leaders on their behalf. Their freedom of action may appear to be restricted by this legacy of the election campaign. They may have obtained what is sometimes called a 'mandate' from the electors for a particular course of action. The nature and validity of a mandate is very difficult to determine. Can it be said that a mandate requires legislators to do what they promised, whatever the circumstances? There can be few legislators who think so. And with what certainty can it be said that a party has a mandate to do all it promised to do? Did all the electors who voted for it, vote for all it promised? Did they all know all it promised? Did not some or many electors vote for it as the lesser or least of the evils submitted to their choice? It would be difficult indeed for a party to say with justification that it was morally or politically justified in doing what it promised, because it had obtained a majority of seats in the legislature, or because it had obtained a majority of votes in the election—the two are not always the same, as we have seen.

The mandate is invoked with some circumspection by legislators. They claim that they have it when they proceed to carry out measures which they like whether or not they promised them at the election. When pressed to carry out measures to which they are opposed, or about which they are uneasy, and upon which they have made no promise to the electors, they reply that they have no mandate from the electorate for such a measure. Opposition parties similarly criticize measures put forward by the majority on the ground that the electors have given no mandate for such measures. And all parties find it preferable to make promises in general or qualified terms so that if they receive a mandate, they will be pledged to do no more than their best in the light of circumstances as they arise. The most that the electors can be said to have decided for certain at an election is who shall sit in the legislature. What else the electors expect the members to do there is much less easy to determine.

The position of the individual legislator who has made promises to the electors or is under instructions from them to speak or act in a certain way is equally indefinite. If he has done no more than promise to advocate some particular measure, then as a rule he will be able to keep the promise. But if he has promised to vote in a particular way, he may find himself in conflict with his party's line. And in any case circumstances may change in such a way that he finds himself unable to carry out his promise. And the sanction available to the electors against him for failing to carry out his promises or instructions may not be very effective, at any rate until the next election comes round. In this respect the electors of the members of the House of Representatives in the United States might be expected to exercise a greater control over Congressmen, for elections occur every two years, than electors of members of the British House of Commons where elections need occur only once in five years.

There is an institution found in some states of the United States whose object is to control the actions of legislators; this is the 'recall'. Upon the demand of a prescribed number of electors, a vote is held to decide whether a legislator should continue in office. If the vote goes against the legislator, his seat is declared vacant and a new election is held to fill it for the remainder of his term. A legislator who had failed to carry out his promises or instructions could thus be deprived of his seat. In practice the power is seldom exercised, and it has not been adopted generally in other states of the Union. There is, also, in some Swiss Cantons a power by which a specified majority of the electors may secure a dissolution of the cantonal legislature before the expiry of its term and this is followed by a new election. This power also is rarely used. Generally speaking electors have no legal means of requiring legislators to carry out their promises or instructions. The attitude in many countries would be that legislators ought not to be given instructions by the electors or required to give pledges to them. It is interesting to find in the constitution of the Fifth French Republic the declaration that 'all imperative mandates are null and void'.

But although legislators may be in a position of ill-defined independence of the electors in the country or in their constituency, their position in relation to their party, nationally or locally is a different matter. Almost all legislators are party men. Their selection as candidates has been controlled by a party organization, national or local or both. How far do party organizations outside the legislature control the actions of the legislators once they have been elected? Do they watch over their actions regularly and strictly? Do they instruct them how to vote on issues as they arise? There is very great variation in this matter from party to party, from country to country and from time to time. A few examples can be given of different types of relationship.

Some parties—and the Communist Party is a good example—control the actions of legislators belonging to their party. The work of the members in the legislature is subordinate to the party organization outside the legislature. It is common for Communist members of a legislature to have placed their resignations, undated, in the hands of the party organization, when they are elected. A similar guarantee is required of the legislators belonging to some socialist and labour parties. Arrangements of this kind conflict obviously with the declaration quoted above from the constitution of the

Fifth Republic, which states, in effect, that they are legally unenforceable.

Then there are parties, of which the Conservative Party in Britain is an example, where the party outside the legislature does not control the party in the legislature. Though the national party organization is not ignored by any means, it is none the less treated as subordinate. Policy is decided by the party in the legislature, or, more accurately, by its leaders. Discipline is provided by the leaders in the legislature, not by a party organization outside the legislature exercising control over members inside. Legislators may not be instructed by the party organization about how they are to vote. It is for the party in parliament, not for the party outside parliament, to decide what is to be done. The resolutions of a Conservative Party conference are not binding upon the party in parliament. They may be treated with respect; they may prove influential; but they are not mandatory.

Just where the British Labour Party stands in this matter is not always quite clear. Its leaders when in office, including Mr. MacDonald, Mr. Attlee and Mr. Morrison, have all asserted that they do not regard the resolutions of the Labour Party conference as instructions to a Labour government in office. And it seems clear that Mr. Gaitskell takes the same view. On the other hand many supporters of the Labour Party do not agree with this view and would accord to the resolutions of the party conference a binding effect upon the parliamentary Labour Party in office or in opposition. What is certain is that the Labour Party conference and its resolutions are taken much more seriously by the parliamentary Labour Party than are the resolutions of the Conservative Party conference by the Conservative leaders in parliament.

But what about the control exercised by a local party organization? Here again there are great differences. Generally speaking, however, their greatest control over the legislator is the threat not to re-adopt him as a candidate at the next election. Save in such parties as the Communist where resignation may be compelled, there is as a rule no power in local party organizations to force their member to give up his seat before the expiry of his term or to vote in a particular way. They may criticize and exhort, but they cannot compel. In other words, they have no power of 'recall'.

Yet the pressure which local party organizations may bring to bear upon a member can be most effective. After all, the threat to disown the member, and to refuse to nominate him for re-election is a very strong power. Members will take care not to allow themselves to get into such a position with their local party. It is only in extreme cases of political dispute that such a situation will arise. There have been such cases in Britain, for example, and members have defied their local and national party organizations, sometimes with success, sometimes not. In a matter where circumstances differ so much from country to country and from party to party it is difficult to generalize. It is tempting to say, for example, that, generally speaking and allowing for individual exceptions on both sides, Conservative members of parliament in Britain are less under the control of their national and local party organizations than are Labour members; that Congressmen in the United States (i.e. members of the House of Representatives) are more under the control of their local party organizations than are Senators: that state legislators in the United States are not so free as national legislators; that legislators in France, once elected, are less liable to control by national or local party organizations than the British or Americans; and so on. But there would be many exceptions to these generalizations. There are American Congressmen and Senators who control their local party organizations; there are Conservative members of parliament in Britain who have lost their seats through a dispute with their local organization, and there are Labour members who have their organization well under control; there are French Communist legislators who act as the party outside requires. Granted the desire of a legislator to stay in office, it is certain that he will do his best to meet the wishes of his local party organization, and if he differs from them will try to persuade them to his point of view. Normally it is not possible to say that the one controls the other; each operates upon the other, and the trial of strength or the showdown is exceptional.

2

Legislators keep in touch with their local party organizations and with the local electorate by visits, not only when the legislature is in recess, but also while it is in session. The extent to which this is done varies from country to country. The British member of parliament spends many week-ends in his constituency; some members have regular 'surgeries' to which constituents are encouraged to come with their problems; others have less formalized arrangements. Contacts are not confined to electors of the member's own party;

they are open to all constituents. They provide him with an opportunity of knowing how people in his electorate are thinking and feeling, while at the same time he can discover from his party supporters and organizers what attitude they take to the issues under discussion. American Congressmen maintain close links with their districts. They start off with an advantage in this respect from the requirement that they must be resident in their district if they are to qualify for election. The locality rule ensures that they have contacts with the community which they represent. Moreover, the fact that they are elected for a short term of two years makes it important that they should keep closely in touch with political conditions in their district. They regard themselves principally as representatives of the district; if they speak for it, press its interests and obtain redress of its grievances, they have fulfilled their task as Congressmen.

It is usual to find a similar close contact between legislator and electors in European countries. In Sweden the locality rule which applies to members of the lower house and by custom increasingly for members of the upper house, emphasizes the link. Most Swedish legislators are in their constituencies at weekends. To assist the member to keep in touch with his constituency most European countries provide free travel, at least between the seat of the legislature and a member's constituency and sometimes more widely.

In countries where the electorate is organized in single member constituencies contact between a member and his constituents would seem easier and more effective than in a country of multi-member constituencies. Members could keep in touch with their

local party organization and party enthusiasts in
multi-member constituencies, but beyond this it
would seem difficult to go effectively. On the other
hand a member who drew much of his support from
a particular part of a multi-member constituency might
be able to maintain contact with that part. Generally
speaking, however, the system of multi-member constituencies, which proportional representation requires,
renders more difficult any close contact between the
member and his constituents.

The size of a country must obviously affect the extent to which legislators can keep in touch with their
districts. In large countries like the United States, or
Canada or Australia or India it will not be possible,
even with air travel, for the same close contact to exist
during the sessions of the legislature as is possible in
the smaller countries of Europe. But if the legislator
cannot get to the constituency, the electors can get in
touch with him. The letter and the telegram play an
important part in the process of influencing the legislators. The letter to the member of parliament is
regarded in Britain as an effective way of having a griev-
ance investigated. Members treat their correspondence
seriously. A question in the House of Commons may
result from a letter from a constituent, and this is a
serious matter. In the United States, usually, the
threat to write to a Congressman is not without effect.

Letters and telegrams are used, moreover, as a means
of expressing local opinion about political policies and
not merely to air personal or particular grievances.
Electors are urged from time to time to write or tele-
graph to their representative and express their approval
or disapproval of policies. This method of influencing

legislators is most highly developed in the United States, where shoals of letters and telegrams pour into Washington with the object of persuading or dissuading Congressmen. These communications are not always spontaneous. Often they have been organized by a body anxious to produce popular support for their point of view. None the less they are not without effect upon American Congressmen, though the weight which they attach to such outpourings will vary a good deal according to their estimate of their spontaneity.

A particular example of this method of influencing legislators is the presentation of petitions. Signatures are collected in support of a project or a protest and presented either to a member of the legislature or by him to the legislature itself. The object is to indicate the strength of opinion upon the particular matter, and at the same time to arouse public interest and to encourage discussion. Most legislatures are prepared to receive petitions—though the Irish parliament does not. What the effect of such petitions is upon legislators is difficult to estimate; it seldom appears to be very great. Yet the practice of petitioning the legislature is actively pursued in some parliamentary countries in spite of meagre results. The fate of a petition when presented to the House of Commons in Britain, for example, looks discouraging. It may be referred to briefly by the member presenting it in the House but no debate is permitted upon it. Or it may be deposited in a bag behind the Speaker's chair. Petitioning the House of Commons is not a fruitful activity.

Associated with the petition as a means of influencing the legislature is the march. Petitioners sometimes march with their petition to the seat of the legislature;

marchers need not, but sometimes do, bring a petition
with them. But a march is a more formidable weapon
than a petition and most legislatures take steps to protect themselves against the impact of marchers. No
legislature is prepared to tolerate intimidation by
marchers, and it is usual to find special provisions in
the law concerning assembly near the legislative
chamber. An example in Britain is the Seditious
Meetings Act of 1817, which makes meetings of more
than fifty persons unlawful assemblies if they are held
within one mile of Westminster Hall when either house
of parliament is sitting. A sessional order of the House of
Commons also requires the Commissioner of Police of
the Metropolis to ensure free passage for members to
and from the House. Though special provisions of this
kind are not found in most countries, police and military protection of the legislature occurs on the basis of
the ordinary law. Marchers are kept at a safe distance
from the chamber and a few selected representatives
alone may be permitted to convey the petition or the
views of the marchers to the legislature.

Another method of influencing the legislature is the
'sit-down', which may or may not be associated with a
march, and if so associated may come before or after
the march. Here similar considerations of public order
apply. A sit-down is an obstruction, and a sit-down in
the vicinity of the legislative chamber obstructs the
work of the legislature.

Legislatures are also made aware of the views of the
electorate by what are usually called public opinion
polls. There has been a good deal of criticism of them
on the ground that they are inaccurate or misleading
or dishonest, and that such influence as they have is

therefore bad. In so far as they provide an accurate assessment of what the electorate thinks upon political issues, they would appear to be doing for the legislator what he tries to do for himself when, by keeping in touch with his constituents, either by visits or otherwise, he attempts to find out what they think about policies. To this extent, then, one might expect legislators to welcome the work of the pollsters. There are, however, certain differences. One is that the results of the poll are published, so that opponents as well as supporters are aware of what is being said and thought. A legislator's discussions with his own constituents are private and do not provide ammunition for his opponents. This difficulty can be overcome, of course, by engaging a pollster to undertake a private survey of opinion and make the results available only to the party or individual employing the pollster.

Whatever justification there may be for criticizing the accuracy and integrity of certain public opinion surveys, it is certain that the results produced, whether published or kept private, influence legislators. This is not surprising, for they supply, or purport to supply just the information which most legislators wish to have—namely what does the electorate think of what is being done or what it is proposed to do. The effect of the information upon legislators will vary. An unfavourable response from public opinion will lead some legislators to take fright and retreat; it will lead others to stand and fight back. This is no new thing in politics; these reactions occurred when less 'scientific', though not necessarily less accurate, methods of discovering public opinion were all that were available to legislators.

3

Some of the methods of influencing the legislature which have been mentioned imply the existence of organized groups whose function it is, though not necessarily exclusively, to try to influence legislators. It is worth while to consider the activities of these groups, for they play an important part in the working of legislatures. They vary a great deal in scope and methods, and it is necessary to distinguish between them if their effect is to be properly understood. They include trade unions, employers associations, professional and vocational associations, groups devoted to the promotion of some object which they believe to be in the public interest, or in their own interest. Sometimes their sole function is to influence legislators; more often the influencing of legislators is only one among many of the ways in which they seek to promote their interests; sometimes they can achieve their objects more effectively by seeking to influence the government rather than the legislature. Most of these organizations are permanent, but others come into existence for a particular purpose and go out of existence when their cause is won or lost.

These organized bodies, regarded from the point of view of their function of exerting influence, are often called 'pressure groups' or 'lobbies'. The name 'lobby' is derived from the fact that the activities of the groups are often carried out in the 'lobby' of the legislative building, where members can be met and talked to. 'Lobbying' is the expression used to describe the meeting or contact with members and talking to them. The word has developed a wider usage and now covers the whole range of activities, including entertainment, which is carried on in order to influence legislators. 'Lobby' is now used to describe the body which exerts influence. There has been a transference in meaning of the word from describing the place where influence was sought to be exercised to the persons or interest or organization which seeks to exercise it. A great part of the process of exercising influence is now carried on outside the legislative building by letter and telegram, by entertainment, by meetings and discussion. Nevertheless, interviewing legislators in the lobby of the legislative building is still an important part of the technique of exerting influence.

One particular aspect of the organization of the lobby which deserves mention has developed, for example, in the United States. As the country is so large, and as the capital city is by no means the industrial or commercial capital of the country, it is necessary for organized interests to set up in the capital regular and permanent offices and representatives to look after their affairs so far as they may be affected by governmental and legislative actions. The headquarters of these bodies may be in large centres of population—New York or Chicago or San Francisco—or they may have several regional headquarters. What they need in Washington is an organization to watch their interests. There has grown up, therefore, a collection of lobbies of this kind, whose sole task is to look after the interests of their organization. In a smaller and more centralized country, like Britain or France, where the political capital is also the industrial and commercial capital, or where it is within easy reach of these capitals, organized groups on a national scale will normally have their head offices in the capital and will carry out a variety of activities there, including the function of influencing government and legislature. No separate, specialized office is required.

In large countries, where the political capital is not also the commercial and industrial capital, the process of influencing legislators raises its own particular problems. If, as in Australia, members tend to flee from the capital at the week-end, then some measure of influence can be exerted upon them in their constituencies. But this will not be enough. Representatives of interests will have to pay frequent visits to the political capital to press their views upon members. These are inevitably intermittent and expensive in time and money. There comes a time when it is thought better to set up a representative in the political capital to keep in touch with legislature and government, to be on the look out for difficulties, to exercise such influence as he can, and to call up the heavy artillery from the real centres of population and power when occasion demands. What has already developed far in Washington is gradually developing in Ottawa and Canberra.

4

By what methods do these organized interest groups influence the legislature? One method is to finance the election to the legislature of members to represent the interest. How far this is done is always difficult to determine. There are some open and acknowledged examples in Britain. The trade unions 'sponsor' candidates, which means, in financial terms, that they pay the whole or a large part of their election expenses. When these candidates are also trade union officials, the union will pay them a salary. In the General Election of 1959, there were 129 Labour candidates sponsored by the trade unions, and 92 of them were elected. The Labour Party in Britain, as in Australia and New Zealand has an open link with the trade unions, and illustrates the extreme case where organized interests influence the legislature by actively forming or playing a large part in a particular party. The link between Conservative parties and organized interests is not so openly displayed, but it undoubtedly exists. So also is the association between the Catholic Church in European countries and the Christian Democratic parties, or between the agricultural and pastoral interests in Australia and the Australian Country Party. These interests can exercise an important influence on parties; they can contribute to their funds and can support members by financial contributions. How far this is done, however, is almost impossible to discover. It is often essential that support be discreet and private, if it is to be effective.

Without going to the extent of sponsoring and financing members of the legislature, however, an organized interest can have spokesmen among the legislators. These are members who are ready to watch the interests of the group in the legislature, and to speak on its behalf. They may hold some office in the organization itself; they may be engaged in the same employment. Their interest and its interest may coincide. They may, for example, be teachers or doctors or business men or miners or local councillors or company directors, and they are ready and able and eager to act as spokesmen for their organization. They are briefed from time to time on questions that arise, and they in turn may pass on information to their organizations. In this way in most legislatures certain members are recognized as the spokesmen of certain interests, though they do not fall into the class of sponsored members whose election has been financed by the interest group.

It is not always necessary for a group to have recognized spokesmen nor to confine itself to them. It may have the services also of members who are ready to be kept informed of a group's views and to speak or act on their behalf from time to time. A group may be able to get in touch with well disposed members who are likely to sympathize with their views because of some professional or business affiliation or through some constituency interest. Groups may have a regular list of such members, or may compile a list from time to time in the light of the issue under discussion. It is clear, however, that members who are doctors or teachers or bankers or local councillors and so on, will be approached by a group if an issue arises where their support would be valuable.

And finally, of course, there are issues upon which a group will think it wise to attempt to influence the whole or a large part of the legislature. On an issue of education, for example, while members who are teachers will be specially approached, all members may be expected to require some lobbying. If a religious issue in education is involved, different methods of approach to different groups of members may be required. Some may be given material for speeches, others may be circularized, others may be called in to discussion on strategy, others or all may receive letters and telegrams and petitions from their constituents at the instigation and by the organization of the interest group. These are familiar operations in all parliamentary countries.

5

The extent to which organized groups, and indeed the ordinary individual elector, will seek to influence the legislature and will, in fact, succeed in so doing, depends in some measure upon the system of government in a country. It will depend, for example, upon how important the legislature itself is within the system of government, in relation, say, to the executive, to the cabinet or president, or to the civil service. In countries where the cabinet controls the legislature—as in the United Kingdom and in many members of the Commonwealth—it will usually be more worth while for an organized group to exercise its influence upon the executive branch of the government. If ministries and ministers can be persuaded to take action that is often all that is needed. As a result, in the United Kingdom, the greater part of the activities undertaken by groups wishing to exercise influence on government is directed towards the executive, in meetings or correspondence with officials and, when necessary, with ministers. There are occasions, of course, when approaches are made to the members of parliament, but these can rarely hope to be effective unless the ministry is ready to co-operate. The exercise of influence upon legislators is, as a rule, supplementary to action upon the executive or it may occur as a last resort when action with the ministries has failed or has not gone well.

An illustration of the same point is found in the fact that most of the approaches made to members of parliament in a system where the cabinet is strong, are made with the intention not that the member shall raise the matter in Parliament, but that he should approach the ministry or minister concerned and seek satisfaction.

In a cabinet system where the cabinet is not so strong as in the United Kingdom, however, a different position obtains. The legislature is relatively stronger and the executive is more sensitive to pressure from it. It is, therefore, more worth while for groups to seek to influence legislators, for they carry more weight with ministers. This is the position in the parliamentary systems of European countries. At the same time, of course, attempts to influence the executive itself will be made in appropriate circumstances.

When we come to a system of separation between legislature and executive, as is found in the United States, the position is that groups will usually find it more worth while to seek to influence the legislature than the executive. At any rate there will be a whole range of matters, including the making of laws and the raising and spending of money, where the legislature has a wide degree of independence of the executive, and groups which seek to influence this area will concentrate their activities upon legislators. They will not neglect the executive entirely, but quite often their main concern with the executive will be to persuade him to veto some bill which the legislature has passed in spite of their lobbying organization. On the whole this is the position that appears in the national government of the United States and in the governments of the fifty constituent states of the Union. It does not seem to be an exaggeration to say that the greater stress placed upon lobbying the legislature in the United States than in the United Kingdom is the result principally of the separation of powers.

At the same time, however, one must not jump to the conclusion that in all countries with the cabinet system influence will be exerted more on the executive than on the legislature. This may be found in countries like the United Kingdom where the cabinet is strong. As was said already, the same is not true in countries where the cabinet is less strong. It is necessary, in fact, to look beyond the actual balance of power between cabinet and legislature to the factors which determine this balance. One important factor is the nature of the party system. Where there is a multi-party system and a coalition government, the legislature has more influence upon the executive, and it will be more worth while to seek to influence it. Or where, even without coalition government, party discipline in parliament is loose, there is greater scope for influencing legislators. What they say will have an effect upon the executive; they will not be required to toe the line. This can be found not only in countries like France where there is a history of unstable cabinet government and where legislatures can be influenced to throw the cabinet out, but also in countries with a stable cabinet system, like the Scandinavian countries and the Netherlands, where party discipline is not rigid and where there is a tradition of compromise and concession between legislature and executive.

And so also in the United States, it is not only the separation of powers which makes the legislature a target for constant lobbying; it is also the nature of American parties. Their nature may indeed be what it is partly because of the system of government in which they operate; but, whatever the reasons, American parties—state and national—have loose discipline and such discipline as exists is created and operated within the legislature not by or from the executive. To say that in Britain legislators vote by party and that in the United States they vote by pressure groups is an exaggeration, but it is probably no more than an exaggeration.

It has been argued, too, that differences of electoral system affect the extent and methods of lobbying of legislators. Where proportional representation with multi-member constituencies exist, it is likely that each member for a constituency feels less beholden to individual constituents or parts of the constituency. In a single member system, on the other hand, pressure is likely to be exercised upon the one member, and the interests of a smaller district can make themselves felt. This is said to be one reason why Swedish members of parliament are relatively free from the pressure of organized interests in their constituencies. It is asserted that this represents a change from the position when single member constituencies existed in Sweden.

Nor should such a seemingly trivial point as the size of the legislature or the size of the majority of the party in office be neglected. Where the legislature is small, every vote counts. It is possible and worth while to influence twenty members in a house of 150 or 200; it may not seem worth it in a house of 400 or 600. If an impression is to be made on a large legislature a much greater effort is required. Similarly, when a government has a small majority, it will be sensitive to the views of its supporters in the legislature, and it is then worth while for an organized group to influence even a small number of those supporters, for they will carry much more weight than they would if the government had a large majority.

The exercise of pressure upon legislatures will be affected also by the way in which the legislature organizes itself to carry out its functions. If a legislature breaks itself up into a series of committees, and if these committees have an important say in what measures are placed before the legislature, and if they have functions of inquiry and investigation, including the taking of evidence, then organized groups will find it worth while to seek to influence these committees. They may be accorded opportunities of placing their views before the committees and advocating or opposing measures which affect their interests. This use of committees is found in the legislatures of the United States and of many European countries; it is seldom encountered in the legislatures of the Commonwealth where committees of the legislature are, as a rule, subordinate in power to the cabinet, and play a minor role. As a result organized groups have much more scope in American and European legislatures through their activities in bringing pressure to bear upon committees of the legislature. And indeed they are encouraged to make their opinions known to the committees, part of whose function is to hear the views of those who favour or object to a measure or course of action.

These committees carry out part of the function which in the United Kingdom for example, is confined to royal commissions, committees of inquiry and other types of advisory bodies. Organized interests are expected to present their views to these bodies; they are sometimes represented upon them; they are regularly consulted upon issues of legislation or administration. Where advisory bodies of this kind are used freely, then the target at which pressure from organized groups is aimed moves away from the legislature. And as most of these advisory bodies are established to advise the executive in Britain, the influence which organized groups exercise, will be directed towards the executive not the parliament. It is only occasionally in Britain that the legislature sets up a select committee of inquiry to report to it upon some matter of public policy and on these rare occasions organized groups have an opportunity to express their views. For the rest, although they may think it worth while sometimes to lobby members of a standing committee dealing with a Bill after its second reading, their efforts are governed by their knowledge that the last word upon what is going to go into the Bill rests with the majority party leadership. They will be better employed in trying to convert the minister or the ministry to their point of view.

The extent to which organized groups will seek to influence the legislature is affected, therefore, by the extent to which other bodies exist in the country whose function it is to provide opportunities for the views of the organized groups to be expressed and transmitted to the seats of power. Where there is a system of non-parliamentary advisory bodies, there is no need for so great an effort to be made to influence the legislature, or it may, perhaps, be made at a later stage if this is necessary. Where committees of the legislature themselves perform these functions of inquiry and advising, attention is correspondingly concentrated upon them. In most countries there is a combination of both systems, but generally speaking in the United States and in European countries, the committees of the legislature play the major part in these functions; in Britain and in Commonwealth countries their role is subordinate to that of advisory bodies, whose advice as a rule is asked for by and delivered to the executive, not to the legislature, at any rate in the first instance.

6

What limits are set to the pressure which outside interests and persons may exert upon legislators? Legislatures differ in their attitude to this question. All would agree in accepting certain limits. Bribery is usually illegal; assault and battery as an instrument of influence would similarly be ruled out. They might occur, but they would be against the rules. When these crude weapons are excluded, however, there is considerable difference of degree in what is and is not permitted in attempting to influence the legislators.

At one extreme stands the parliament of the United Kingdom which reacts quickly and strongly to any suggestion of undue influence on or intimidation of a member. It regards any such action as a breach of the privilege of freedom speech for members of parliament. Such a breach of privilege amounts to contempt of the House of Commons or of the House of Lords, as the case may be, and the House is itself the judge of a breach of its own privileges and can itself punish an offender. It is a breach of privilege to molest any member of parliament on account of his conduct in Parliament, or to attempt to influence members in their conduct by

threat, or to reflect in speech or writing upon his conduct as a member. Thus it was held by the House of
Commons, in 1934, that a breach of privilege had been
committed in a letter to members wherein the writer
had set out a list of questions referring to proposed
legislation to make certain sports illegal, and had
intimated that, if he did not hear from such members,
he would feel justified in letting their constituents
know that they had no objection to cruel sports.

The House of Commons has adopted a strict view
also concerning the relations of a member to any body
which has sponsored or supported his candidature.
It resolved in 1947 that 'it is inconsistent with the
dignity of the House, with the duty of a member to his
constituents, and with the maintenance of the privilege
of freedom of speech, for any member of this House to
enter into any contractual agreement with an outside
body, controlling or limiting the member's complete
independence and freedom of action in Parliament or
stipulating that he shall act in any way as the representative of such outside body in regard to any matters
to be transacted in Parliament; the duty of a member
being to his constituents and to the country as a whole,
rather than to any particular section thereof'. And the
Committee of Privileges, in this case, remarked that
'the relationship between a member and an outside
body with which he is in contractual relationship and
from which he receives financial payments is, however,
one of great difficulty and delicacy, in which there must
often be a danger that the rules of privilege may be
infringed'.

The power of the two houses of the legislature in the
United Kingdom to punish for contempt of themselves

is a strong power and is by no means a dead letter. It acts as a restriction upon the press and the public in their freedom to criticize the conduct of members of the Houses. It is not possessed by any European legislature. It is found, however, in the parliaments of most of the members of the Commonwealth, including the legislatures of the states of Australia, the states of India and the provinces of Canada. It has not been used so freely or so strictly as in Britain. Though a few cases of complaint against persons who are alleged to have committed contempt of a legislative house are raised on an average each year, most of them are dealt with by apology or explanation and no question of the imposition of a penalty by the chamber arises. When two persons were imprisoned for contempt of the Australian House of Representatives in 1955, this was the first occasion upon which that House had used its power since it had been established in 1901. The Indian House of the People used its power to punish for contempt for the first time in August 1961 when it reprimanded the editor of a weekly newspaper which had published a violent attack on a member of the House. It may be that the existence of the power is sufficient to prevent occasions that call for its exercise. It seems more likely, however, that more freedom of speech in criticism of legislators is regarded as tolerable in most Commonwealth countries than by the British House of Commons. When it is sought to curb criticism of the legislature in Commonwealth countries it is, in any case, more likely to be done by the enactment of repressive legislation than by resort to the power of the legislature to punish for contempt.

Apart from the legislatures of the Commonwealth, it

is mainly in the United States that one finds the power of punishment for contempt exercised from time to time. Indeed its exercise by the House of Representatives, or more usually, by investigating committees of the House, particularly the Committee on Un-American Activities, has led to a great deal of controversy. These cases, however, do not fall within the class which are being considered at the moment. They concern contempt arising from a refusal to answer questions put by members of the committees. We are considering the use of the power to punish for contempt when a person has threatened or otherwise exercised undue influence upon the legislature. The power of the American Congress to punish for contempt in this way was regarded as essential for the performance of its functions though not specifically granted in the Constitution. It has, however, been rarely used. Here again it seems certain that public opinion expects and tolerates much greater freedom of speech towards politicians in the United States, as in many Commonwealth countries, than is permitted by the House of Commons in Britain.

The principal method by which American legislatures seek to defend their members against undue influence or pressure is, however, by the enactment of laws regulating the activities of lobbyists. They require lobbyists to register and to declare for whom they are acting; in some cases they are required to declare what expenses they have incurred in their lobbying activities. Some state legislatures prohibit the arrangement by which a payment is made to a lobbyist if the legislation which he is supporting or opposing is passed or defeated, as the case may be.

There is a great deal of discussion in the United States about the wisdom and effectiveness of these anti-lobby laws. Even if lobbyists are registered, their activities are not curbed or abolished. Nor is it clear that they should be. Bribery and intimidation, needless to say, are against the law, and it is difficult to see how the registration of a lobbyist will add anything significant to these restrictions. Lobbyists are active in federal and state legislatures, and indeed commonly carry out their activities in state legislatures not merely in the lobby of the legislative building itself, but also upon the floor of the houses themselves. State legislatures have made rules against these intrusions, but it is clear that in most cases little attempt is made to enforce them. It is permissible to doubt whether most legislators in the United States feel the need of being protected against lobbyists.

7

The sources and methods of influence on legislatures described in this chapter operate upon legislators from outside the machinery of government. But one of the most important influences upon a legislature is the executive, the administration or the government. No legislature is uninfluenced by it, though the degree of influence and the methods by which it is exercised vary a great deal. And the extent to which a legislature is affected by the influences which have been described in this chapter will itself depend upon the nature of the influence which the executive exerts upon the legislature. It is this relationship which we must consider now.

Chapter Four

MAKING THE GOVERNMENT

I

WHEN Walter Bagehot was writing about the House of Commons in his book *The English Constitution* nearly a century ago, he said this: 'The House of Commons is an electoral chamber; it is the assembly which chooses our president'. And he added: 'The elective is now the most important function of the House of Commons.' When Bagehot wrote this he had in mind the method which the Americans had devised in their Constitution for choosing their chief executive. They had provided for what is usually called an electoral college—though it is really a collection of electoral colleges, one chosen in and for each state by the voters of that state—whose task it was to choose a president. It was intended that the members of the electoral college should really deliberate on this matter and elect the man who, in their opinion, was most suitable for the post. In practice, as is well known, party entered into the process quite soon and the electoral college became a collection of pledged party men whose choice for president was already declared. Once it was known which party had an absolute majority in the electoral college, it was known who was going to be president. This was what it was like when Bagehot wrote and this is what it is like today.

But what Bagehot was saying about the House of

Commons in his day was this. The House, he said, really does do what the American electoral college was intended to do by the founders of the American Constitution. The American plan had miscarried. In the British House of Commons you found a body which 'is a real choosing body; it elects the people it likes. And it dismisses whom it likes too.' The Prime Minister and his cabinet are in office because they have the confidence of the House of Commons and they lose office when they lose that confidence. And he expresses this paradoxically by saying: 'It is the Assembly which chooses our president.'

It is hard to say how true this was as a description of the role of the House of Commons in making the government in Bagehot's day. What is true is, that you can use Bagehot's phrase today but you must give it a different meaning. The electoral college which the House of Commons resembles today is the sort of electoral college which in practice the Americans soon had and now have. Once you know after a general election in Britain, that a party has an absolute majority in the House of Commons, you know who the Prime Minister will be. In the process of making the government, the House, like the American electoral college of today, is a transmitting body, a recording body, almost a scoreboard upon which you can read the result of the game. In this matter of making the government—which is quite distinct from making the government behave or unmaking it—the House of Commons today, like the American electoral college does not deliberate. It registers a result, and it is itself a result of a decision transmitted by the electorate.

There the comparison between the two bodies ends.

What happens after that is so different that it may seem to some people that it renders the comparison invalid. The members of the American electoral college go home, their powers exercised and exhausted; the members of the House of Commons stay, and they stay to support, to advise, to criticize, to give consent, and, occasionally, to unmake the government. As for the American legislature, it has no say in the choosing of the President—save in the rare case (it happened in 1801 and in 1825) where no candidate for the Presidency obtains an absolute majority in the electoral college, and the choice falls to the House of Representatives. But as a general rule the President, unlike the Prime Minister, holds office whether or not he has the confidence of the members of the legislature; and what is more they hold office whether he likes them or not. They and he have their fixed term, so that neither can force the other to go back to the electorate before their time. Moreover, their terms vary in length—House of Representatives two years, President four years, Senators six years, with a third retiring every two years—so that it is not only possible but common for the legislature and the President to belong to different and opposing parties for part at least of the presidential term. And finally, while the Prime Minister and the cabinet must be members of parliament, neither the President nor his cabinet may be members of Congress.

This distinction between the British system of making the government and the American system is well known, and it is a classic distinction. It is expressed sometimes by saying that the Americans have the separation of powers and that Britain does not; or, again, that the Americans have the presidential or non-parliamentary executive and that the British have the parliamentary executive. And the British system is commonly called 'cabinet government'. These distinctions are undoubtedly very important, however difficult it is to describe them accurately or intelligibly, and political scientists are not wrong in dividing the world of representative democracy into two parts. There are, on the one hand, those countries in which, putting it generally and roughly, the legislature, in some sense and to some degree or other, makes the government; there are, on the other hand, those countries in which it does not.

But what we have to remember is that once that division has been made, still further sub-divisions have to be made, certainly inside the group of the countries that have the parliamentary executive or cabinet government. Indeed, the more we study it, the more it seems that some systems of cabinet government differ from each other, and especially from the British, quite as much and quite as significantly as the British system differs from the American. In saying this one is not thinking only or mainly of the French system of the parliamentary executive, although we shall deal with it inevitably. There are, indeed, more startling differences to be found in other and less notorious examples.

2

Let us begin with a proposition which, it may be asserted, people in Britain regard as fundamental to the cabinet system. They would say that cabinet government means not only that the cabinet holds office for so long as it has the confidence of the House of Commons, but also, and equally important, that the heads of the government, the ministers, must be members of parliament, of one house or the other. There is in Britain no law which requires this; it is required by constitutional convention only. There can be, and have been, occasional exceptions.

In Commonwealth countries the same rule applies. Canada relies, as does Britain, upon convention to enforce the rule. Others, such as Australia, Nigeria and India, lay it down in their constitutions that ministers must be, or must within a specified short period— usually three months—become members of the legislature. New Zealand, since 1950, forbids by law the appointment as a minister of a person who is not at the time of his appointment, a member of the House of Representatives. In the Commonwealth it would be generally agreed that cabinet government could not work otherwise.

Yet when we look at cabinet systems in Europe, what do we find? In Norway, the Netherlands, and the Fifth French Republic, ministers are expressly forbidden to be members of the legislature. If they are members, they vacate their seats on appointment, and their places are taken by substitutes, elected at the same time for this very purpose. Surely, one would think, this is the separation of powers on the pattern of the United States. But there is a difference and it is an important difference. For although in these countries, as in the United States, ministers may not be members of the legislature, yet, in contrast to the United States, they hold office because they have the confidence of the legislature and they lose office when they lose that confidence. What is more, ministers are allowed and, indeed, expected to sit in the chambers of the legislature and speak there, though they cannot vote. Norway, the Netherlands and the Fifth Republic thus provide a curious mixture of the parliamentary and non-parliamentary executive.

This raises the question of just what it is that is the essence of cabinet government. Is the dependence of ministers for office upon the confidence of the legislature enough, or must they also be members of the legislature? In practice the systems in Norway and the Netherlands at any rate—the Fifth Republic is *sui generis*—do conform to the essentials of cabinet government as understood in Britain and the other Commonwealth countries, for ministers have a place though no vote in the legislature; they may have been members of it immediately before taking office; and they may stand again for election to it at a general election, relinquishing membership again when they take office.

Norway and the Netherlands illustrate in an extreme way a characteristic of cabinet government as it works in continental Europe, which can be best described not as the separation of powers, not as keeping the government out of the legislature, but as keeping the government at arms length in the legislature. And this is true generally of other continental legislatures even when they do not forbid ministers to be members of the legislature—on the contrary, in these countries most ministers are, by custom though not by legal requirement, members of one or other house of the legislature. Yet there still survives, in greater or less degree, a constitutional dualism accepting the independence of legislature and executive. It is symbolized, for example, by the reservation of a special row of seats for ministers, usually in the front row of the centre of the semi-circular chamber, and there they sit apart. Though some of their supporters may be sitting behind them, there is no guarantee of this; it depends upon the party composition of the legislature. They do not sit, as in Britain and most Commonwealth countries, backed by the concentrated numbers of their supporters. Ministers in the Netherlands chambers seem particularly isolated. While members face each other in the rectangular chamber, and speak from the rostrum, ministers sit at a special table at the far end of the chamber facing the presiding officer, and they speak from there, not from the rostrum.

And there are other examples of their isolation. Ministers in France and Sweden, for example, may not be members of the standing committees which consider legislation, though they may be invited to attend their meetings, and usually are. This seems odd to British practitioners of cabinet government who expect a minister not only to be a member of a committee but in effect to be the driving force of it.

And yet there are some factors on the other side. Although continental legislatures hold their cabinets at arms length, in varying degrees, they give them in one respect a measure of encouragement to take part in the proceedings of the legislature which is denied to British members. Continental countries permit their ministers to speak or take part in the proceedings of both houses of their legislature, instead of confining them, as in Britain, to that of which they are members. And even in Norway and the Netherlands, where ministers may not be members of either House, they are permitted to speak in both. In the Commonwealth though some countries follow the British practice—Canada is an example—in others, such as India, ministers may speak in both houses.

3

Although some features of the working of the parliamentary executive in Norway and the Netherlands may seem odd to practitioners of cabinet government in Britain or other Commonwealth countries, there is no doubt that it is what happened in France under the Third and Fourth Republics which strikes them as most interesting and notorious and mysterious. There, they feel, you can see just how cabinet government could go wrong. There is Walter Bagehot's electoral chamber. The French National Assembly of the Fourth Republic, like the Chamber of Deputies of the Third was 'a real choosing body; it elects the people it likes. And it dismisses whom it likes too.' There were about 100 changes of government under the Third Republic, and there had been about twenty-five when the Fourth Republic was superseded in 1958. Making the government, and, even more, unmaking the government and remaking it, was the principal occupation of the French legislature. And we may contrast its actions with those of the British House of Commons or legislatures in other Commonwealth countries which may, in general terms, be said to make government by registering the decision of the electorate. When the electorate's opinion is not asked for in Britain, it is as a rule on such occasions of crisis as that of 1940, when Mr. Chamberlain's government was unmade by the House of Commons and Mr. Churchill's was made by it. In normal times that action by the House of Commons would have been referred at once to the electorate for approval or disapproval.

We must be careful, of course, not to push the contrast too far. Although the British House of Commons resembles the American electoral college in registering and reflecting a decision by the electorate concerning the making of government, it does have some effect upon the choice of who will be in that government. The House of Commons exercises what Harold Laski called 'a selective function'. This function is difficult to describe and its working is somewhat mysterious. Put crudely, office in Britain is obtained and retained to a large degree by success in the House of Commons. The Prime Minister is, after all, the leader of the majority party in the House of Commons, and he and his colleagues justify what they do before the House. While it is true that in Britain the electorate decides which side shall have the government, who is to be Prime Minister and who is to go into a cabinet are decided, in some measure impossible to determine precisely, by the opinion of the House of Commons.

The matter is taken even further in some Commonwealth countries. In Australia, for example, though here again the legislature registers a decision of the electorate as to which side will form the government, if that side should be the Labour Party, it is the members of that party in the legislature who decide which of its number shall be in the ministry. They ballot and give their leader the names of those he must appoint, leaving it to him to allot them to their respective offices. And in the Republic of Ireland we find a provision in the Constitution whereby the Prime Minister must submit his list of proposed ministers to the legislature and receive their approval, before submitting it to the President.

It must be understood, therefore, that while in Britain and in most Commonwealth countries, the legislature does not make the government in the sense in which the continental legislatures do so and in particular as the French chamber did under the Third and Fourth Republics, it has a certain influence, varying in degree, in the allocation of office, once the electorate has given its answer.

4

But one need not quarrel with the custom of holding up the French system of cabinet government as a contrast to the British. It was a contrast and a most instructive contrast. But let us be clear about the respects in which it was a contrast. It was a contrast between unstable cabinet government and stable cabinet government; it was also a contrast between weak and strong cabinet government. At the same time let us remember that the French system was a contrast with other continental systems. Far from being typical of continental cabinet systems, the French came near to being exceptional. Most other continental legislatures, when they make a government, maintain it. They resemble the French legislatures of the Third and Fourth Republics in that they really do make the government but they resemble the British in that they really do support it once made.

The experience of the Netherlands illustrates this point extremely well. After a general election in the Netherlands, it is seldom obvious which parties are to form the government. Prolonged consultations take place. And when cabinet crises occur they are often of extremely long duration. In 1925 the formation of a cabinet after the elections took over two months; a ministerial crisis which began in November of that year lasted for 113 days; there was a crisis for fifty days in 1951 and for sixty-eight days in 1952. In 1956 a record period of 122 days elapsed after the general election before a new government was formed. Meanwhile, the old government continued in office handling business, including important issues such as the Suez crisis, with no apparent difficulty. Holland without a government did not seem so helpless as France without a government. Yet the number of days occupied in cabinet crises in Holland matches and probably surpasses the French record. The difference is that once governments have been formed, they have been more stable than French governments. It has been usual for a Dutch cabinet, when finally formed, to last for the duration of the term of the legislature. The number of individual crises is smaller and they do not always result in a change of government. Between 1918 and 1940, only three different persons were Prime Minister, although in that period there were eight cabinet crises. From 1946 to 1956, there were four cabinets, but only two Prime Ministers, each of whom when not Prime Minister, served in the cabinet of the other. And the crisis of 1956 was resolved by the formation of a cabinet under the previous, i.e. the outgoing Prime Minister.

It would be as foolish to suggest that the Netherlands is typical of European countries in the relation between its legislature and its government as it is to suggest that France is typical. Clearly the system in the

Netherlands is in many ways individual and different. But in one respect it is typical and that is in the degree to which it provides an example of the stable and moderately powerful cabinet system. For in the Scandinavian monarchies of Norway, Sweden, and Denmark, and in Finland we find a similar record of stable and moderate cabinets. In Belgium and Italy there is a lesser degree of stability, but if we consider Belgium since 1918 and Italy since 1945, though there have been periods of instability, their record still places them nearer to the class of stable cabinet system than to the instability of the French system under the Third and Fourth Republics. And if we are to make comparisons with Britain since 1918, it is well to remember that in 1922 the coalition government under Mr. Lloyd George was overthrown and succeeded by a Conservative government first under Mr. Bonar Law and then after a few months under Mr. Baldwin; that this Conservative government was succeeded in 1924 by a minority Labour government under Mr. Ramsay MacDonald which fell after nine months, to be replaced by a Conservative government again under Mr. Baldwin; and that in 1929 Mr. Baldwin's government was defeated in the general election and a further period of Labour minority rule, under Mr. MacDonald, occurred until 1931. Britain has had its periods of instability.

Preoccupation with the contrast between the French and British way of making and unmaking government has tended to establish the view that if you have an unstable cabinet system you have a weak executive like the French and if you have a stable cabinet you have a strong or dominant executive like the British. But while there can be little doubt that if cabinets come and go frequently, they will be weak in relation to the legislature, it does not at all follow that stable cabinets are necessarily strong or dominant. And a study of continental legislatures, other than the French, illustrates this. The characteristic of these stable cabinets is not that they dominate, lead and control the legislature as a British cabinet does, but that they work with it more as partners, as equal and distinct (though not separate) authorities. It would be misleading to call them 'weak' cabinets, more particularly in the context of the weak French cabinets of the Third and Fourth Republics, though in relation to the British cabinet they are weak. They are best described perhaps, in terms adapted from the weather reports, as moderate, moderate to strong, and even moderate to weak. Norway, Sweden, Denmark, and Finland have provided many examples of moderate and moderate to strong; Belgium and Italy, perhaps, quite a number of examples of moderate to weak.

This distinction between the system of the stable cabinet and the system of the strong cabinet is important. It helps us to understand how some legislatures in Europe view their relations with the government and vice versa. Cabinets do not expect to have their own way on everything; they compromise and concede, they accept amendments. They do not make every detail a matter of confidence. And so, by this process of give and take, legislatures and cabinets live together. But notice the contrast not only with the French system of the Third and Fourth Republics, where the legislature dominated the cabinet, but also with the British where the cabinet dominates the legislature. It is sometimes asserted in Britain that if the government began making concessions to the House of Commons, the country might end up with the system of unstable government which France had before the Fifth Republic. Is it not conceivable that it might end up with something more like the system of stable though moderate cabinets which some other legislatures in Europe support?

When we look at the relations between the legislature and the executive in European countries, we are forced to the conclusion that it is the French system of the Third and Fourth Republics and the British system which are the exceptions. Britain with its stable, dominant cabinet, and France with its unstable, weak cabinets contrast not only with each other, but with the stable, moderate cabinets of other parliamentary states in Europe. And even if the aims of the makers of the Fifth Republic are realized, and France achieves a stable and strong cabinet system, France would still be exceptional. And it may be added that among Commonwealth countries it is by no means invariable that the British system of the dominant cabinet will be found. There are examples of the stable but moderate cabinet in Commonwealth countries—Canada and Australia are examples—and there are examples of unstable and weak cabinets, of which Ceylon has provided examples.

It is important to remember always that each country's system of government, and in particular each cabinet system, has its own individual or unique features. It would be foolish to suggest that we may lump together the systems of Norway, Sweden, Denmark, Finland, Belgium, and Holland as if they were all much the same, just as it would be foolish to lump

the Commonwealth countries together. For the purposes of exposition it is necessary to speak of European
or continental legislatures or systems of government,
but it is important to remember that such language can
mislead. Each of these legislatures differs from the
other in striking ways, some of which have been already
mentioned, and more will be exhibited in later chapters
as we study their working. At the same time, so far as
stability and the moderate cabinet system is concerned,
the European countries we have mentioned have a
certain amount in common and it deserves notice.

5

None the less, in Britain people have no belief in,
or sympathy for, the system of the weak executive,
even though it be joined with stability. Neither of the
two leading political parties in the country intends to
govern in that way. They might consider that it is a
suitable system, or at any rate a possible system, for
small states of a few million people, to be governed by a
cabinet which is continually giving way to the legislature. They feel inclined perhaps to adapt the words
which Mr. Kenge, the lawyer in Charles Dicken's novel
Bleak House, used to Mr. Jarndyce when he spoke in
defence of the Court of Chancery: 'We are a prosperous
community, Mr. Jarndyce, a very prosperous community. We are a great country, Mr. Jarndyce, we are
a very great country. This is a great system Mr.
Jarndyce, and would you wish a great country to have
a little system? Now, really, really!'

Yet one great country, the United States, has
deliberately chosen the moderate and stable executive.
Though an American President may not be able to get

his own way with Congress, he has his fixed term of office. The consequences of this separation of legislature and executive seem odd to British eyes. In terms of effectiveness in carrying the legislature with him, most American Presidents are weaker than a weak British Prime Minister; while a weak American President is weaker than any British Prime Minister could possibly be, for he would have lost office long before. The strength of the American President in relation to Congress may be described as moderate, and varying from moderate-to-weak to moderate-to-strong. Such a deliberate arrangement to ensure that the legislature may thwart the executive seems indefensible to British eyes, but there are few Americans who are prepared to see it changed.

If we are to understand this point of view we have to get used to the fact that in some countries, and the United States with its great size and divergencies is a leading example, you must govern with a loose rein if you are to govern at all. The choice lies not between stable strong government and stable moderate government, but between stable moderate government and unstable weaker government, ending up in no government at all. A fixed term for the executive, rendering it independent of the legislature in its tenure can ensure that a government will be in existence. It is not surprising perhaps that in the discussions about constitutions in some Commonwealth countries there were those who urged the advantage of the American type of executive with its stability as against the cabinet system with its dangers of instability which the French system has made so notorious.

Nor should we forget the interesting compromise

between the parliamentary and non-parliamentary executive which Switzerland has operated for so long. Its legislature—the two chambers voting together—chooses the executive after a general election, and to this extent ministers can be said to hold office because they have the confidence of the legislature. But once elected not only do they cease to be members of the legislature—as happens in Norway and the Netherlands also—but they hold office for the fixed term of four years, the life of the legislature. It is to these devices for ensuring a stable and moderate executive that political and social conditions in some countries have directed the attention of constitution makers.

There are people who believe that a strong executive, even if you can have it, is a bad thing. They think that executive power tends to corrupt, that it is easily abused. They think that there are, anyhow, strict limits upon what government should do; that government is a necessary evil and therefore the less you have of it the better. This point of view is strong in the United States and in France, where executive dictatorship is considered to be a dangerous possibility. To the British observer, used to the firm leadership of his cabinet system, nothing seems less likely in these countries.

It is natural to ask why it is that legislatures occupy such different positions in different countries in the process of making the government. The question is easier to ask than to answer. It is likely that there is a different answer for each country. Some general explanations are offered which it is worth while to consider.

It is suggested, for example, that the existence of a

multi-party system, encouraged, if not actually created, by proportional representation, has a good deal to do with it. Where there is a multi-party system, a general election is less likely to produce a legislature in which there is one party with an absolute majority and where the government is clearly designated. The legislature itself, therefore, has an important part to play in making the government. The inter-party discussions that follow a general election in the Netherlands is a good example. Where, on the other hand, there is a two-party system, as in Britain, the electorate chooses the party which is to form the government, and the legislature registers the result. Its part in the process though not negligible, is much less that it is in countries like the Netherlands or in the Scandinavian countries.

This explanation takes us some way. It helps us to understand why Britain has a dominant cabinet and why some European countries have a moderate cabinet. But it does not entirely explain differences of stability. Why should the multi-party system produce cabinet stability in the Netherlands and the Scandinavian countries, say, and instability in France? Why do the multi-party legislatures in the former countries, having played a large part in making the government, thereafter support it, whereas the history of the French legislature in the Third and Fourth Republics is an account of the making and unmaking of cabinets? Clearly the multi-party system can be used as a basis for a stable moderate cabinet system or as an opportunity for creating cabinet instability and consequent weakness in the executive.

And to bring proportional representation into the

explanation does not in fact help us very much. If we allow that proportional representation encourages a multi-party system, we find that in France that factor is almost irrelevant, for proportional representation has been used there for short periods only. The multi-party system and cabinet instability have been rife at times when there was no proportional representation. And on the other side, there has been a history of stable cabinet government in Ireland, and in many states on the continent of Europe under a system of proportional representation.

Then it is said that the existence of a power in the executive to dissolve the legislature assists cabinet stability. It is maintained that one of the reasons why a British cabinet dominates the House of Commons is that, at the sign of any trouble from his own party, the Prime Minister can threaten a dissolution. Party discipline, so lacking in the Third and Fourth Republics, is maintained in Britain by the threat of dissolution. To this it must be said, first, that stability is achieved in some European systems without the dissolution. It is not available in Norway; its use in Sweden is severely limited by the fact that a house elected after a dissolution continues only to the end of the normal four-year term. Dissolution is not regarded by the executive in Sweden as a weapon to discipline the parties.

But is it indeed so regarded in Britain, in spite of what is said to this effect from time to time? If a cabinet in Britain is having trouble with its party, how could it be helped by going to the electors at such a time? A party divided within itself is hardly in the best position to seek a renewal of the electors' confidence. The 'weapon' of dissolution in Britain, is, in fact, used by a Prime Minister against the Opposition, either to choose a favourable time for an election, within the limits of what is regarded as political decency, or to try and resolve a situation in which the opposition is pressing the government hard and the only way out is to seek support from the electorate. It is true that the threat of dissolution has an effect upon party discipline in Britain but it is not the result of a threat by the Prime Minister to his own party. If the leaders of the government party in Britain are faced with rebellion in their party and a possibility of being defeated by a defection of their supporters, they can say to the rebels: If you vote against the government and it is defeated, we shall have to resign; the opposition will take office; they will dissolve parliament; and we will face the electorate as a divided party. This is not a threat, but a plea. This argument may cause the rebels to toe the line. It may also cause them to reply: If the government is defeated, it will not be our fault; it will be yours, because of the policies you are pursuing. If you modify the policies, we will toe the line. And discussions and compromise may follow. The matter is indeed much more complicated than is suggested by those who believe that the Prime Minister's power of dissolution keeps his party in line. Party discipline in Britain, in fact, is founded upon the power of a party in the last resort to refuse to adopt a 'rebel' member as a candidate at the next election. The stable dominant cabinet in Britain may be explained more in terms of party organization than of the power of dissolution.

There is one general explanation sometimes offered in particular for the instability of French cabinets and the stability of British and of other European cabinets and that is the explanation of differences of national character. This explanation, it can be said, itself calls for more explanation than it offers. It is sometimes thought almost frivolous. But it has been put forward by the author whose words were quoted at the start of this chapter. Walter Bagehot wrote about French government when he was a young man in his twenties. He contributed a series of seven *Letters on the French Coup d'Etat of 1851* to *The Inquirer* in January 1852. His comments on French politics at the time when the Second Republic was overthrown and the Second Empire inaugurated with a strong executive under the Prince President Louis Napoleon, later Napoleon III, are interesting to read at a time when the Fourth Republic has been overthrown and a Fifth Republic inaugurated with a strong executive under President de Gaulle.

A principal theme in these *Letters* is that the French are really too clever for stable parliamentary government. Nor does he stop there. He goes further and explains why stable government exists in Britain. 'What I conceive to be about the most essential mental quality for a free people', he wrote, 'whose liberty is to be progressive, permanent and on a large scale is much *stupidity*.' And he adds: 'I need not say that, in real sound stupidity, the English are unrivalled.'

When one reads Bagehot's account of French politics, written more than a century ago, one begins to feel that, whether there be a French national character or no, there are certain enduring French political traditions where the working of legislatures is concerned. His description of the way in which the legislature of the Second Republic set about its tasks fits

exactly the record of the legislatures of the Third and
Fourth Republics. French legislatures could only be
understood by Englishmen, Bagehot thought, if they
tried to conceive of an House of Commons composed
of all Disraelis. Nowhere in the French legislature was
there 'any steady majority, any distinctive deciding
faction, any administering phalanx, anybody regularly
voting with anybody else, often enough, or in number
enough, to make the legislative decision regular, consistent or respectable. Their very debates were un-
seemly.' This has quite a modern sound about it. And
the explanation he offers to us is that the system is a
natural and inevitable result of the French national
character. 'If you have to deal with a *mobile*, a clever, a
versatile, an intellectual, a dogmatic nation', he says,
'inevitably, and by necessary consequence, you will
have conflicting systems—every man speaking his own
words, and always giving his own suffrage to what
seems good in his own eyes—many holding today what
they will regret tomorrow—a crowd of crotchety
theories and a heavy percentage of philosophical non-
sense—a great opportunity for subtle stratagem and
intriguing selfishness. . . .'

This explanation may seem far-fetched, at first sight,
but it may have more sense in it than others. Stable
cabinet government, whether it be of the strong British
type or of the moderate type found in Scandinavia or
the Netherlands owes much to certain habits of mind
and character which work institutions in a particular
way. And if we find rather less cabinet stability in
Belgium and Italy, may not their national characters,
comparable more to the French than to the Dutch
and Scandinavians, offer some part of the explanation?

'Stupidity', is a harsh word; Bagehot apologized for it, but he praised it as 'Nature's favourite resource for preserving steadiness of conduct and consistency of opinion.' It meant 'the continual application of sensible heads and pliable judgements to the systematic criticism of stiff axioms, rigid principles and incarnated propositions'. And so he concludes: 'Nations, just as individuals, may be too clever to be practical, and not dull enough to be free.' Whatever value we attach to his explanation based on national character, Bagehot's words express vividly the qualities which are necessary in a legislature to produce stable cabinet government.

Chapter Five

MAKING THE GOVERNMENT BEHAVE

I

WRITERS on politics sometimes engage in the pastime of considering which country has made the most important invention in the art of government. The Americans would certainly have a strong claim with their invention of the device of federalism, which has been adopted and adapted so freely in Europe, in Latin America and in the British Commonwealth, where, since the Second World War, it has been very much in fashion. The Swiss cannot perhaps claim that they actually invented the referendum but they made it into a practical instrument of government which they, at least, know how to handle successfully. Admirers of the French system of administration might claim that in the two institutions of the prefect and of the *Conseil d'Etat* France has devised instruments for the co-ordination and control of executive action which deals with problems either left untouched by other countries or dealt with far less adequately. For Britain several claims can be made. There is the institution of the parliamentary executive, or cabinet system; there is the Civil Service, described by Graham Wallas as 'the one great political invention in nineteenth-century England'. Alongside these two great inventions one other may be placed—the institution of the Leader of Her Majesty's Opposition. A famous American, Lawrence Lowell, professor of government at Harvard, and later president of the University, wrote in his *Government of England*: 'His Majesty's Opposition embodies the greatest contribution of the nineteenth century to the art of government'.

We need not settle an order of merit in these matters; we can easily concede that the invention was important. Indeed, it is not too much to say that in the British Constitution today the office of Leader of the Opposition is regarded as of no less importance—though it may be less desired—than that of Prime Minister. There was a striking illustration of this in Britain in 1937. In that year it was decided, at long last, to make some provision for paying a salary to the Prime Minister. For decades it had been almost the glory of the British Constitution that no salary was paid to the Prime Minister as such. It was true that, as a rule, the Prime Minister also held the office of First Lord of the Treasury and received a salary—quite a small salary —in respect of that office. Not all Prime Ministers held that particular office—in Lord Salisbury's third government, formed in 1895, for example, the First Lord of the Treasury was Mr. A. J. Balfour, but Lord Salisbury was Foreign Secretary and could draw a salary in respect of that office. But by 1937 it was thought desirable to regularize the practice and incidentally to pay a more appropriate salary to the holder of the chief ministerial office in the country. And this was provided for in the Ministers of the Crown Act of 1937. In that same Act—and here is the significant thing—it was also provided that a salary should be payable to the Leader of the Opposition. When the British came to consider paying a salary to the Leader of Her Majesty's Government, they thought straight-away of the necessity of paying a salary also to the Leader of Her Majesty's Opposition. In the same act of parliament and for the first time both offices are recognized as of fundamental importance in the system of government.

But the Mother of Parliaments was not the first legislature to recognize in this way the important role of the Leader of the Opposition. Two at least of the daughter nations in the Commonwealth had anticipated her. Canada was the first—probably the first in the world. As far back as 1905 the Canadian House of Commons decided to pay a sessional allowance to the Leader of the Opposition. Sir Wilfrid Laurier, Prime Minister at that time, said: 'The Leader of the Opposition under our system is just as much a part of the constitutional system of government as the Prime Minister himself.' Australia was next, when in 1920 a salary was provided for the Leader of the Opposition in the House of Representatives, though already in the state legislature of New South Wales, at least, a salary had been paid to the Leader of the Opposition since 1912. So, long before Britain accepted the principle of paying the Leader of the Opposition, it had become established in the Commonwealth—but not every-where, since New Zealand, for example, did not adopt the principle until as late as 1951.

There are, incidentally, two respects in which, in the Commonwealth, the principle has been carried further than in Britain. First of all it is recognized that leading the Opposition in the upper house of the legislature deserves some additional remuneration. This was pro-vided for in Australia, for example, at the same time as the Leader of the Opposition in the House of Representatives was given an allowance. In Canada it came later—it was not until 1947 that the Leader of the Opposition in the Senate was given remuneration for his duties. In Britain, however, the Leader of the Opposition in the House of Lords gets no salary.

The second interesting departure found in some Commonwealth countries is the recognition of the leaders of minor opposition parties as deserving some remuneration. In Australia, for example, since 1947 an allowance may be paid to the leader of an opposition party with not less than ten members in the House of Representatives.

But although in Commonwealth countries these differences are found in the application of the principle of paying leaders of the opposition, it is accepted in these countries, as in Britain, that, in so far as one of the functions of a legislature is to make the government behave, the chief part in performing that function falls to the Opposition and its Leader. It is important to stress that they are not expected to undertake the whole of this task. The government's supporters are not supposed to be mere yes-men; influence can be exerted from outside the legislature, as we explained in Chapter Three, by individuals or by organized interests, which help to keep the government up to the mark. But in the legislature itself, though government supporters may grumble behind the scenes and occasionally in public, it is the members of the Opposition who are charged with the duty of examining and criticizing what the government has done and proposes to do. Through questions to ministers in the House, through motions of censure and no confidence, through the debates that accompany the passing of financial legislation and so on, the Opposition in the British and in other Commonwealth legislatures carries on its task. And the leading idea upon which it is organized is that it offers itself before the country as an alternative government. It criticizes upon the understanding that, given the opportunity, it could do better itself. In this way, so runs the theory at least, it is possible to have not only responsible government but responsible Opposition also. The Opposition criticizes upon the understanding that it is prepared to take the consequences of its success.

In Commonwealth countries, this pattern is familiar. Indeed, we are inclined to take it for granted. But we should not. There is nothing inevitable or automatic about it. To begin with, to speak of *Her Majesty's* Opposition is no mere flourish. It means much more than that opposition is permitted or even that it is legal. It means that it is constitutional; that it is 'loyal'; that though the Opposition may disagree with the government on important matters, it agrees with it on the rules of the game. It means that some fundamental questions are outside the party fight. There is agreement about the régime, about the form of government. Now not all countries have a party system of this kind. In some countries there are deep differences about the very fundamentals of the constitution. Some parties do not accept the rules of the game; they work to get them changed. The Communist and monarchist parties in France and Italy are in this position, and Communist and extreme right-wing parties in many other European countries similarly do not accept the existing régime. And when Lawrence Lowell described

Her Majesty's Opposition as the greatest contribution of the nineteenth century to the art of government, he justified his statement on this very ground that it meant that parties could now disagree because they had a basis of agreement upon the constitution. Things were not always like this in Britain. Differences about religion and about the régime in past centuries had made it impossible to speak of opposition parties as Her Majesty's Opposition. They were not loyal; they were rebellious, disaffected, even seditious.

There is a second point. A system of responsible opposition of the kind we are discussing can only exist and be effective if in fact the Opposition has a chance. It must have some hope of winning, or at least of increasing its strength. How can it criticize responsibly if it knows or feels and everybody knows and feels that it can never be more than an ineffective minority, a voice in the wilderness? But in some countries where opposition parties are based on, say, some religious or linguistic or national difference, they have in fact a fixed following, but little chance of increasing it. And even without this restricted basis of party organization, there come times in a country when a government is so long in power that the Opposition loses heart and seems to have no prospect of success. In such countries there is really no responsible Opposition; it is not an effective instrument for making government behave. It can easily become irresponsible, factious, desperate. These are not unknown situations in parliamentary countries, nor, in a sense, are they anybody's fault. Nor is it easy to see how, with the best will and political sense in the world, they can easily be avoided or readily be cured.

2

But let us take this question of the prerequisites of responsible opposition a little further by asking this question: Who is the Leader of the Opposition in the United States? There is a government of the United States and there is plenty of opposition to it, and plenty of people leading and anxious to lead this opposition. But there is no one official Leader of the Opposition. The Americans have a two-party system; one party has the presidency and the other party offers itself as an alternative, ready to provide a President from its side. But who is he? Nobody knows, except for a period of a few months once in every four years when presidential election campaigns are held. Opposition in the United States, as in Britain, is permitted, is legal and is 'loyal'; both parties are united in reverence for the constitution. There is so much resemblance yet there is no Leader of the Opposition.

What about Congress? There is plenty of opposition there to what the administration does and proposes. Congress is indeed a principal organ in the United States for making the government behave. It investigates administration, it uses to the full its power of the purse to obtain redress of grievances before it votes money. In this task many powerful men in both Houses of Congress take a lead; they are not confined to one party, as is usual in Britain. After all, since Congress cannot throw the government out, as in a system of cabinet government, every Congressman is freer to express his views and to vote against the President's proposals. Opposition can be less responsible for it will not inevitably have to take the consequences. And members of the President's own party have a freedom of action which is denied to government supporters under the British cabinet system. They can defeat the government without destroying it. In the end it is the separation of powers which enables the legislature in the United States to exercise enormous authority in making the government behave, while at the same time it exercises this authority through no one responsible Leader of the Opposition.

The American system often bewilders people in Britain and in other Commonwealth countries. If there is a Leader of the executive in the United States, why is there no Leader of the Opposition? And when various leaders speak in criticism of the administration, who is to be taken seriously? When is criticism 'official' criticism? To questions like this, the American is entitled to answer. 'In looking for a Leader of the Opposition in the United States, you are looking for something you are not entitled to find. For, after all, there is no Prime Minister in the United States, and consequently there is no Leader of the Opposition.' And there is, of course, a great deal in this. The Leader of the Opposition is a parliamentary leader, just as the Prime Minister is, and he is a product of a system where ministers hold office because they have the confidence of the legislature and lose office when they lose that confidence. We cannot expect, therefore, to find the leader of the American opposition in Congress, for the President is not there either. All the same it is odd that in some way the Americans have not devised a system by which the party out of office in the White House would have a leader in the country, the rival of the president, and the leader of opposition to him.

In practice many men offer themselves for this task, with an eye to the party's nomination as presidential candidate, and constitute themselves as leaders of opposition, but whether they will be the official party candidate when the contest comes remains to be seen.

But, if to look for a Leader of the Opposition in the United States is to exhibit one's misconception of the American Constitution let us turn to some countries which have the system of the parliamentary executive. What about France? Is there a Leader of the Opposition in France? There again, as in the United States, there is plenty of opposition and plenty of people leading it. And there is a Prime Minister. But there is no one official Leader of the Opposition. The reasons here are different from those in the United States. It is not wrong to look in the National Assembly of France to find a leader of the opposition. But the multi-party system, the loose discipline within the parties and groups, and the existence of certain groups which cannot form a government or will not join a government means that no one party or group stands forth under a leader offering itself as the alternative government. Under the Third and Fourth Republics, indeed, the successor to a French Prime Minister was often not only inside his own party but inside his own cabinet, or he was found in some small group of available men who led no party at all. In France, as in the United States, though for different reasons, while the legislature exercised very great powers in making the government behave, it performed that task through no responsible opposition with an official leader. Although the powers of the legislature to control the government are less under the Fifth Republic, the situation so far as leadership of the opposition is concerned is substantially the same.

And France is not alone in this position. To a great extent in continental legislatures where the legislature makes the government, where, after an election, the legislature has some room for negotiation about who shall form the government, it is rare to find the institution of Leader of the Opposition as it is understood in Britain and the Commonwealth. No one acknowledged 'pretender' to the prime ministership is recognized as a rule in these parliamentary systems. Here the multi-party system has its effect as in France. But the moderation and compromise, the atmosphere of give and take, which marks the relations of ministers and legislatures in the Low Countries and Scandinavia must also be part of the explanation. To venture a generalization, the institution of the leadership of the Opposition, as understood in Britain and in the Commonwealth today, is essentially the product of a system where the legislature does not make the government but where it registers or transmits the decision of the electorate about making the government. The leadership of the Opposition, like the prime ministership, is an institution in the country as well as an institution in parliament.

3

It is in the light of these general considerations upon the pattern of opposition in different countries that we can now consider in rather more detail some of the methods and instruments which are used by legislatures in their attempt to make the government behave. First of all let us consider the use of questions, that is to say, asking a question of the government in a full session of the legislature. Obviously this instrument of control is not available to legislatures in countries where, as in the United States, the executive is not present in the legislature. It is found in countries where the parliamentary executive is adopted, though the extent to which it is used, and used effectively, varies a good deal.

It is in Britain that the parliamentary question achieves its greatest effectiveness as an instrument for making the government behave. On each of the sitting days, except Friday, an hour is set aside for oral answers to questions. In addition there is provision for written answers. So popular is the asking of questions that restrictions have been placed upon the number which members may ask—since 1960 no more than two may be put down for oral answer on a particular day by a member. (There is no restriction upon the number of questions which may be put down for written answer.) And all questions, whether for oral or written answer, must be submitted in writing. Moreover there are strict rules about the admissability of questions to ensure that they are relevant and not repetitious, rules which the Speaker of the House and the clerks must apply. In spite of these restrictions, however, there is seldom time on any day for an oral answer to be given to all the questions put to ministers. On an average between eighty and ninety questions are put down for oral answer each day and only between forty to forty-five are given an oral answer. The rest are either postponed or given a written answer. When it is remembered that, at the discretion of the Speaker, members (including members who did not ask the original question) are permitted to ask supplementary questions, the small proportion dealt with in the time is less surprising. In a normal session of the House of Commons about 11,000 questions for oral answer are set down on an average each year and about 5,000 are given an oral answer. About 3,000 questions a year or a daily average of about twenty are set down for written answer and receive it. All questions receive some answer, even if it is not always very revealing, though it is within the competence of a minister to refuse to answer.

In the other countries of the Commonwealth and in Ireland provision for the asking of questions for oral or written answer is usually found, but it has not always achieved the same effectiveness as in Britain. In the legislatures in Europe the rules regulating the asking and answering of questions differ in some interesting respects from what obtains in Britain. In Denmark, for example, a questioner is allowed up to five minutes in which to explain the purpose of his question, and he may ask a supplementary question, but other members are not allowed to join in. In Norway also the questioner alone may ask a supplementary question. In Sweden the questioner and the minister who has answered him may debate the answer, but there can be no general debate unless the chamber permits it, and this it rarely does. In Italy the questioner is allowed to speak for five minutes after the minister has answered his question.

The number of questions answered orally in European legislatures is very small. In Belgium, indeed, questions may not be answered orally except in case of urgency. In France, under the Fourth Republic, about seventy questions were answered orally each year and this represented about half the questions asked for oral answer. Although the constitution of the Fifth Republic provides that, at one sitting each week, priority shall be given to questions from members of the legislature and answers to them by the government, it seems unlikely that the number of questions answered orally will increase. (Questions are in fact questions with a short debate and may be followed by a vote.) The experience of the Netherlands has been that, as ministers are not members of the legislature, though they may appear in the chambers, it proves difficult in practice to question them orally. It would not be surprising if in the Fifth Republic, where ministers similarly are not members of the legislature, the same situation arose.

The use of the power to ask questions for written answer seems also to be used sparingly in European legislatures, with the possible exception of the Fourth French Republic where about 4,000 questions a year were asked for written answer in the National Assembly. In the Netherlands, for example, the annual figure in the lower house is round about 200; in Sweden the number in the lower house is usually under forty. This relative neglect of the question as a means of controlling the administration is not easy to explain. But part of the explanation in Sweden, Finland, and Denmark is the existence of the office of *Ombudsman*, or parliamentary commissioner, whose task it is to receive and investigate complaints from citizens about the administration. These officers deal with a great number of the matters which, in Britain, for example, would provide the content and occasion for a question in the House of Commons. It is conceivable, too, that in some European legislatures, members may prefer and may indeed find it more effective, to raise questions privately with ministers or ministries, rather than to resort to the somewhat restricted and artificial form of a question.

A small part of the explanation why the use of questions appears so slight in some European legislatures, is, however, the existence of an institution which is really a question in origin, but something more also. This is the interpellation, which is used in most European legislatures, but is unknown in the legislatures of Britain, other Commonwealth countries, or Ireland. The interpellation is, in effect, a question, often accompanied by a statement, the answer to which can be debated, and may, in some legislatures lead to a vote. When in Sweden, for example, the chamber allows the debate between the questioner and the minister on the answer to an ordinary question to become general, it is converting the question into an interpellation, though it may be noted that in Sweden no vote is allowed at the conclusion of the debate on an interpellation. The use of the interpellation has increased in Sweden in recent decades; it is used in both houses; there were forty interpellations put down in the upper house and eighty-seven in the lower house in 1950. In the Netherlands, on the other hand, the number of interpellations had declined, though it was seldom above ten, and the average is now round about four per year. The interpellation was a powerful weapon in the Third French Republic, but its importance declined in the Fourth Republic. Although the number of interpellations put down was still high, the number actually debated was much smaller. There were, for example, about 350 interpellations put down in 1952, but only seventeen of them were debated by the National Assembly and these were so grouped that there were only three debates. On the other hand, the vote on an interpellation was regarded as a serious matter by a French government; defeat would normally involve resignation. Interpellations were not reintroduced in the Fifth Republic, though the practice of permitting a short debate on oral questions with a vote to follow was a small concession in that direction.

4

Although in Britain and other Commonwealth countries there is no procedure of interpellation and questions are not allowed to lead to a debate and a vote, methods exist by which a similar result can be achieved. There is provision by which the motion for the adjournment of the House can be used to raise a particular matter, extract a reply from the government, conduct a debate, and, in some cases, proceed to a vote which, though formally a vote upon whether the House is to adjourn or not, is in reality a vote for or against the government. Thus, in the British House of Commons, for example, there is in practice what amounts to an interpellation debate several times a week.

Votes of confidence and censure are used in some European legislatures also, although they are not found in Sweden or Belgium. They are naturally also not applicable in countries like the United States or Switzerland, where the executive's tenure of office does not depend upon the confidence of the legislature, for it is implicit in the notion of such a vote that if it goes against the government, the government must resign. In Britain the government may put down a motion asking the House of Commons to approve its policy and express its confidence in it. Similarly, if the Leader of the Opposition desires to move a vote of censure upon the government, the latter arranges for a debate to be held upon the subject.

Questions of confidence played a large part in the relations between legislature and executive in the Third French Republic and were a regular method by which French cabinets were unmade. When the constitution of the Fourth Republic was framed an attempt was made to restrict the use of the question of confidence, so that cabinet instability might be reduced. The vote of confidence was given a somewhat technical meaning and was intended to be distinguished from an ordinary vote for or against the government. Moreover the vote of confidence was separated from the vote required to permit a new cabinet to take office. A Prime Minister-designate was required to make a statement of his policy to the National Assembly; this was followed by a debate and a vote; if the Prime Minister-designate received the support of an absolute majority of all the members of the Assembly, he was appointed to office by the President of the Republic. In this way it was intended that no government should take office unless it was clear that it had the assurance of support from the Assembly and thus the defeat of a government after only a few days or weeks of office would be avoided.

On the question of confidence itself, it was provided that only the Prime Minister could put it to the Assembly and it was for him to decide therefore, whether or not on a particular issue before the Assembly the fate of the government should be in issue. When the Prime Minister raised the question of confidence, further consideration of the matter was postponed for twenty-four hours. On the vote, an absolute majority of all members of the Assembly was required to defeat a vote of confidence. To emphasize the seriousness of the vote of confidence, and to ensure that the Assembly would be required to think of the consequences of its action, the vote of confidence was linked with the power of dissolution. It was provided that if, after the first eighteen months in the life of a legislature, two governments fell within eighteen months as a result of defeat on a vote of confidence, then the Assembly could be dissolved by the President of the Republic on the advice of the cabinet.

The constitution of the Fourth Republic also introduced the motion of censure which could be moved by any one member of the Assembly. Here again one clear day had to elapse before the motion was debated, and an absolute majority of all members was needed to carry it.

Dissolution, upon the passing of a vote of censure, could occur in the same circumstances as for the refusal to pass a vote of confidence. The vote of censure and the vote of confidence were on an equal footing for this purpose.

There is little evidence to show that these provisions reduced cabinet instability in the Fourth Republic. The Assembly was able to bring about the resignation of governments without the question of confidence being raised by the Prime Minister or a motion of censure being tabled. Cabinets defeated by less than an absolute majority on a question of confidence or defeated by any majority in other votes gave up, though legally they were not required to. As a result, deputies opposed to a cabinet could either vote freely against it on an issue other than a question of confidence or else skilfully adjust their votes on a question of confidence so as to defeat the cabinet by less than an absolute majority. The threat of dissolution had practically no effect. It could not be invoked in the first eighteen months of the Assembly's life. After that time, ministers were not usually anxious to bring dissolution upon themselves and the groups to which they belonged. The vote of censure was seldom employed.

The framers of the constitution of the Fifth Republic had as one of their major aims the strengthening of the executive. They abolished the procedure by which a Prime Minister-designate sought the confidence of the Assembly. Instead a Prime Minister is appointed to office by the President of the Republic. He may then, or at any time, after deliberation with the council of ministers, raise the question of the existence of the government before the National Assembly, either upon its programme or upon a general declaration of policy. If the Assembly disapproves of the programme or the general declaration the government must resign and, it may be noted, an ordinary majority of members voting is all that is required to defeat the government in this case. At the same time it must be emphasized that there is no obligation upon the government to make such declarations at the beginning of its term of office or at any time.

Apart from declarations of programme and general policy, however, the government is regarded as having the confidence of the Assembly unless a motion of censure is carried against it. A motion of censure requires the signatures of at least a tenth of the members of the Assembly; it cannot be voted upon until at least forty-eight hours have passed after it has been put down; and it is not regarded as carried unless there vote in favour of it a majority of the total membership of the Assembly. If the motion of censure is defeated, the signatories to it are precluded from moving a new motion of censure in the same session of the Assembly, save in the following circumstances. The Prime Minister can, again after deliberation with the cabinet, raise the question of confidence on the vote upon a particular text, for example, a particular Bill or part of a Bill. This text is regarded as carried unless a motion of censure is put down within twenty-four hours of the raising of the question of confidence by the Prime Minister and passed in accordance with the rules already mentioned. If the Assembly passes a vote of censure the Prime Minister must submit the resignation of the government to the President of the Republic.

The passing of a vote of censure is clearly a difficult matter; a mere majority of members voting is not enough. Abstentions do not harm the government; only positive votes for the censure motion count. And the defeat of the government is not linked with the power of dissolution. It is for the President of the Republic, after consulting the Prime Minister and the presidents of the two chambers, to decide this question at any time.

Yet it is difficult to judge how far these provisions, taken by themselves, would be effective in reducing cabinet instability in France. The requirement of an

absolute majority to pass a censure motion is similar
to what was required in the Fourth Republic. The
strength of the executive, if it exists, must be supplied,
one would think, from some other source. There are in
fact a number of provisions in the constitution which
make it possible for the government to govern without
the consent of the Assembly. Some mention of the law-
making powers of the government will be made in the
next chapter. The fact that there was cabinet stability
in the first years of the Fifth Republic can be explained
partly by these provisions in the constitution, but
largely by the strength and prestige of President de
Gaulle. With de Gaulle on the scene, it was impossible
to know how the provisions of the constitution would
work. They were almost irrelevant while he was in
office.

The use of the motion for the adjournment as a
means of criticizing the government is practically
unknown in European legislatures, but it is part of the
regular procedure in the legislatures in most Commonwealth countries and in Ireland. In Britain the opportunity can be taken by a member on the motion to
adjourn at the end of the day's sitting, or before
adjourning for a recess. Notice of the matters to be
raised is given to the appropriate ministers. There is in
Britain, Ireland and in most Commonwealth legislatures, too, the possibility of moving the adjournment
of the House to consider a definite matter of urgent
public importance. The permission of the Speaker is
needed for the moving of this motion, and it has been
customary for him to grant this permission rarely.
When such debates have occurred they have usually
amounted to a serious attack on government policy by

the Opposition leadership; and the motion to adjourn is really a motion of censure and the vote is regarded by the government as a matter of confidence.

In some Commonwealth countries, also, there is another procedure for criticizing the executive which is not usually found elsewhere—the debate on the address in reply to the Queen's or, in India, for example, to the President's speech opening each new session of the legislature. In this speech the government's policy is outlined and there ensue some days of debate upon a formal motion thanking the Sovereign for the speech. The debate provides an opportunity for a general discussion of policy in which administration can be considered, and replies are expected from the appropriate ministers when their departments are criticized.

Similar opportunities of general debate are afforded at the beginning of the session in Sweden, and at other times when periodic messages are communicated to the two chambers. The debate on the investiture of a Prime Minister-designate in the Fourth French Republic and on the policy statements of a Prime Minister in the Fifth Republic are comparable. It is interesting to notice that in the Republic of Ireland, where much of the procedure of the legislature follows the British model, the practice of a speech by the head of the state at the opening of a session and a debate on an address in reply to it, is not followed—it lapsed as early as 1924. In the United States, although messages from the President are a regular and important event in the life of the legislature and of the nation, Congress as a whole does not debate them: they are considered by the appropriate committees of the legislature in so far as they propose legislation.

5

Many legislatures find that their most effective instruments for making the government behave arise out of their functions as law-making bodies. They are asked to consider bills and, in the course of doing this, they look into administration. In particular they take the opportunity of financial legislation to find out what use the government is making of money already voted or what it proposes to do with what is to be voted. In most continental legislatures and in the legislatures of the United States also, it is through their law-making functions that legislatures find their principal opportunities to control the executive.

The chief instrument in this work is the committee system. Outside Britain and Commonwealth countries, it is common to find that legislatures set up a series of committees to each of which is assigned a field of governmental activity—foreign affairs, agriculture, trade and commerce, finance, defence, shipping, and so on, and they regard themselves as entitled to find out what the government is doing in these fields. Any Bills that relate to these subjects will, of course, be referred to the appropriate committee. But committees do not regard themselves as confined mainly to the consideration of bills. They question the executive; they investigate departments; in some countries—as in the United States—they call outside witnesses before them to hear their views on administration as well as legislation. By these means the committees can obviously inform themselves in much greater detail than can the individual member asking a question of a minister in the House as a whole.

The nearest approach to the use of this sort of instrument in Britain is found in two committees which the House of Commons sets up to exercise control of the executive in the financial sphere—the Select Committee on Estimates and the Select Committee of Public Accounts. Although committees are used to consider Bills, they are neither in composition nor function comparable to American or European committees. They are constituted *ad hoc*, they are confined to a discussion of the particular Bill before them, and they have no particular field of governmental activity assigned to them. Their nature is well illustrated by the fact that they are designated by letters of the alphabet, A, B, C, etc. It is only in the Estimates and Public Accounts Committees that there is that specialized investigation and study by a small body of what the executive is doing which is characteristic of committees in the legislatures of the United States and European countries.

These two British committees are undoubtedly an effective method of making the government behave. They call officials of government departments before them—they are indeed unusual in this, for it is a general rule in British government that civil servants do not appear before legislators but that ministers alone speak and take responsibility for their actions. In these two committees the practice is reversed—ministers do not appear before them, only civil servants. It is maintained that as these committees may not discuss policy, ministers need not appear.

Opportunities to discuss administration in Britain are not confined, however, to the members of these two select committees. Estimates are discussed also in the House of Commons as a whole, sitting as Committee of Supply, and later in the regular stages of the Appropriation Bill, while proposals for taxation are discussed similarly by the whole House, in Committee of Ways and Means, and later in the regular stages of the Finance Bill. In these debates the Opposition selects topics which it desires to discuss, and although there is not the detailed examination of questions which is possible in a system of small committees, the government's administration is continually subject to discussion and criticism. In the debates on the Estimates, indeed, it is not money so much as administration and policy which is dealt with, with the Opposition itself determining very largely the subjects upon which attack is to be concentrated.

These general debates upon administration in the course of discussing financial legislation are not peculiar to the British House of Commons, of course. They are a regular feature of legislatures in other Commonwealth countries, in Ireland, and in European legislatures (except Sweden). They are an important part of the business of Congress and of state legislatures. They provide an additional opportunity in these legislatures to criticize the government, for they supplement the detailed inquiry that has gone on in committees.

Nor is the use of committees to investigate administration confined in the legislatures to those committees to which Bills are referred. It is the practice in most European legislatures to set up committees to inquire into a particular matter. This is a well-known feature of the way in which the American Congress does its work. In Britain and most Commonwealth countries nowadays the use of a committee of the legislature in this way is rare. It is more usual to appoint some outside body—a royal commission or a committee of inquiry—which might include members of parliament among its membership, but need not.

What is significant, however, is that in Britain and most Commonwealth countries no committee of inquiry is likely to be set up by the legislature unless the government is willing. Congressional committees of investigation in the United States on the other hand are set up if Congress wishes it. The executive may deplore it, but is powerless to prevent it. In European legislatures, similarly, the assembly is usually so independent in relation to the cabinet, that its wish to set up a committee of investigation would not be gainsaid; to attempt to prevent it would be regarded as an unwarrantable interference with the legislature's own affairs. But in Britain the supremacy of the cabinet is usually sufficient to ensure that investigations of the government are carried out only with the government's consent.

6

A brief word may be added about one instrument for making the government behave which is found in some countries, and that is impeachment. This weapon still exists in Britain as a matter of law, but the law is a dead letter. There has been no impeachment for over 150 years. It may be said with some confidence that if the British Constitution was being codified today, it is unlikely that impeachment would be included in it. The penalties available for ministers' misconduct in loss of office or in prosecution in the ordinary courts would be considered sufficient.

None the less impeachment is found in modern, and indeed in quite recent constitutions. The Constitutions of the Fourth and Fifth French Republics contain provisions for impeachment of the President of the Republic in a case of treason, and of ministers for other crimes and offences committed in office. Impeachments are tried by the High Court of Justice which is composed of members elected by the National Assembly and the Senate, from their own members and in equal numbers. An impeachment against the President can be initiated only by the assemblies ruling by identical vote in an open ballot and by an absolute majority of their members. It is interesting to notice that in the Fourth Republic the National Assembly only was required to act, and a secret ballot, not an open ballot was ordained. The weapon of impeachment was not treated as a dead letter under the Fourth Republic. Two or three attempts to initiate impeachment of ministers were made, though none secured a sufficient majority.

In the Indian Constitution of 1950, similarly, there is a provision by which the President of the Republic may be impeached, one house initiating the complaint and the other investigating it. But it is to be noted that this procedure applies not to ministers but only to the President.

When the American Constitution was drawn up provisions for impeachment were inserted, by which the House of Representatives initiates the prosecution and the Senate tries the impeachment. Similar powers are found in state constitutions in the United States. Although it might be thought that the insertion of the power of impeachment in the American Constitution was an eighteenth-century feature of government which would now be out of date, it would not appear to be so. It is true that only twelve cases of impeachment have been tried by the Senate, nine of which involved judges, and one, the most notorious, the President of the United States himself, Andrew Johnson, who was acquitted in 1868. It must be remembered, however, that the American Congress, unlike the British parliament, lacks the power to remove its chief executive by a vote of no confidence, and that it is reluctant, therefore, to give up its only power of removal, namely impeachment. Moreover, so far as the removal of judges is concerned, the American power of impeachment is comparable to the power in Britain and Commonwealth countries by which judges may be removed on the passing of an address to the head of the state by the legislature. At any rate it would be rash to assume that impeachment of a President or of a cabinet officer would not nowadays be undertaken by the American Congress. And it cannot be doubted that where subordinate officers and judges are concerned the existence of the weapon may go far to make its use unnecessary.

7

In assessing the effectiveness of legislatures in making the governments of their countries behave, we start off with the fundamental fact that legislatures are in very different situations in relation to the executive in performing this function. In one sort of situation, of which Britain and some Commonwealth countries provide an example, the Opposition criticizes the government with the knowledge and expectation and hope that it may be called upon itself to take on the administration. In another kind of situation, of which the United States is an example, those who criticize the government are called upon to do no more than criticize. An American Congressman is, of course, responsible to his electorate and his party organization in his own district and is very conscious of the fact, but he is not responsible to them, nor is his party in Congress responsible to them for the conduct of the administration. That is a matter for which the President is responsible.

But, in a curious way, the 'responsible' type of opposition, associated with the British system, and the 'irresponsible' or 'non-responsible' type associated with the American Congress produce unexpected results so far as the effectiveness of criticism is concerned.

In the task of making government behave, there is something to be said against the system of the 'responsible' opposition and something to be said in favour of the 'non-responsible' system. When opposition is really responsible, when it is in danger of defeating the government and being obliged to take office itself, it can become very cautious, it can pull its punches. Shadow cabinets, like real cabinets, must maintain discretion; they must also maintain discipline. The conduct of opposition becomes a front bench matter; the rank and file may not be given a free hand. At times the two front benches, one on each side of the House, may seem in closer sympathy with each other than either is with some at least of its followers on the back benches. Experience of office or expectation of office can make an opposition too well behaved to make the government behave.

This is no more than a statement of a tendency or a trend which shows itself at times under a system of opposition of the British type. By contrast in a system like the American you can get a much freer use of criticism, not only from the side of the party which does not hold the presidency, but also from the President's own party. And why not? For a Congressman can vote against the administration but he will not dislodge it or himself in so doing. In a system like the French in the Third and Fourth Republics, members could defeat and dislodge the government, but that is what they regarded themselves as elected to do—to make and unmake governments. In a system like that in some other European countries where governments and legislators do not take umbrage with each other so easily, and are not constantly raising issues of confidence, the members can criticize the government in the expectation that it will give way or compromise and that no question of defeat or dismissal need arise.

In these European and American systems there seems to be much more scope for examination of what a government is doing. It may be irresponsible; it can become mere obstruction; it can nullify government, as is seen in the United States from time to time; and it can be merely factious and self-seeking, and it can be corrupt. All this is true. And yet with it all there is this to be remembered on the other side—a disappointing and a disquieting fact for those who believe in the system symbolized by the Leader of Her Majesty's Opposition—that in some ways, and in quite important ways, the methods of opposition employed in the United States and in some European legislatures are a more effective instrument for making the government behave.

Chapter Six

MAKING THE LAWS

I

In Britain and the Commonwealth it is usual to speak of 'parliaments'; in the United States and other countries they usually speak of 'legislatures'. This distinction in the use of words represents a real difference—a difference of view about the proper role of representative assemblies in the process of making the laws. Beneath this difference, admittedly, there is certain common ground. Generally speaking, the process of law making cannot be authorized or completed without the consent of the representative assembly. But when we come to consider the process before and by which that consent is obtained, important differences appear. Some of these differences can be illustrated if we put a series of questions about the law-making process in various countries and see what answers to them can be discovered.

2

A first question is: What may the legislatures make laws about? At once we come upon the distinction between those legislatures which are unrestricted in the matters upon which they may make laws, and those which are restricted. The legislature of Britain, for example, is competent to make a law upon any matter it thinks fit. This means that if a Bill is passed by the British Parliament and assented to by the Queen, it will be accepted by the courts as valid. There can be no dispute in Britain about the validity of an Act of Parliament. In the United States, on the other hand, it is possible to raise in the courts the question whether an Act of Congress or an Act of the legislature of any of the fifty states is valid, on the ground that it deals with a matter with which, under the Constitution, the legislature in question is not competent to deal. The same question may be raised in regard to the legislatures of, for example, Canada or Australia or India.

These restrictions upon the subject matter of legislation arise in different ways. In federal systems the restrictions arise because the constitution lays down that some subjects are within the law-making competence of the general legislature of the whole country, and that other subjects fall within the law-making competence of the states or provinces of the country. All the legislatures of the country are thus restricted. This is the case in the United States, Canada, India, or Australia. In some other countries restrictions are placed upon the subjects with which the provincial or regional legislatures may make laws, while the general and central legislature is unrestricted. This is the position, for example, of the legislature of Northern Ireland within the United Kingdom. Another example of this type of system is found in the Union of South Africa, where the legislatures of the five provinces of the Union—the Cape Province, Natal, the Orange Free State, the Transvaal, and South-West Africa—are restricted in their law making to a list of subjects specified in the Constitution of the Union, while the parliament of the Union is not so restricted.

But restrictions upon subject matter do not arise

solely from some territorial divisions of powers between a central legislature and state or provincial legislatures. They may arise from a division of law-making powers within a central or regional government itself, by which, for example, the representative assembly may be restricted to voting laws on certain subjects, and the executive may be authorized to make laws on others. This division is found, indeed, in the Constitution of the Fifth French Republic, and is one of the instruments by which the framers of that constitution sought to strengthen the cabinet and make it less dependent on the assembly. The Constitution sets out a list of subjects which are to be within the province of the parliament. They are certainly important, for they include finance, nationalization of undertakings, the electoral system for parliament and the local authorities, defence, property and civil rights, matrimonial questions, and nationality. What does not come within these headings, however, can be regulated by ordinances made by the executive. And as it is only the general principles of some of the topics enumerated in the list that the parliament is authorized to deal with, the scope of the law-making power granted to the executive by the Constitution is very extensive. A constitutional council rules whether a matter is within the parliament's competence or not.

There is yet another type of restriction upon the power of parliaments to make laws. This arises when a constitution forbids any authority, be it legislature or executive, to make laws on a particular subject or subjects, or to make a particular kind of law. This prohibition may be found in a unitary state just as much as in a federal or decentralized system of government.

Thus the legislature of the Republic of Ireland is forbidden to make laws permitting divorce. No legislature
in the United States is permitted to abridge or deny
the right of citizens of the United States to vote on
account of sex. The Congress of the United States is
restricted in its law making by the first ten amendments to the American Constitution—the Bill of
Rights—so that, for example, it may make 'no law
respecting an establishment of a religion, or prohibiting
the free exercise thereof, or abridging the freedom of
speech, or of the press, or the right of the people
peaceably to assemble and to petition the government
for a redress of grievances'. Private property shall not
be taken for public use, without just compensation.
Neither Congress nor the legislatures of any of the
states may deprive any person of life, liberty or
property, without due process of law. These are
restrictions imposed upon the Congress of the United
States or upon the state legislatures by the Constitution of the United States itself. If we looked at the
constitutions of the several states themselves we would
find further restrictions imposed by them upon their
respective legislatures. Similar restrictions upon legislative power are found in some of the newer constitutions
in the Commonwealth, as in India, Malaya, and
Nigeria for example. Restrictions of this kind arise
because people believe not that a particular subject
should be regulated by a central legislature rather than
by a state legislature, nor that it should be regulated by
the legislature rather than by the executive, or *vice
versa*, but because they believe that no legislature, be it
central or state, should legislate upon such matters.
They may hold that such laws would be contrary to

the rights of the subject or to good morals or to
religion.

One final restriction as to subject matter may be
mentioned. It is common to find that laws amending
the Constitution itself are placed beyond the uncon-
trolled competence of a legislature. This is a natural
restriction. It is the purpose of a constitution to establish and regulate the system of government, including
the legislature, and it would seem proper that the
legislature itself should not be made superior to the
instrument which created it.

3

There is a second question which may be asked.
Looking at legislatures in general—who decides what
Bills they shall deal with? The short answer to this
question in Britain, in other Commonwealth countries,
and in Ireland and South Africa is: the government.
This does not mean that the government has a completely free hand. For one thing there are some Bills it
has to introduce whether it likes it or not—Bills to
raise money and Bills to spend money. And there are
some Bills it might like to introduce but it dare not
because its supporters would not stand for them. In the
matter of introducing Bills, as in everything else, a
government in these countries, by definition, must
carry its supporters with it: it must continue to com-
mand their confidence. But bearing all this in mind, the
substantial power to decide what Bills the legislature
is to consider lies in the government. Every government
(except that of Ireland) is expected to announce at the
beginning of a session, in the Queen's Speech, or its
equivalent, at the opening of parliament, a general

outline of the Bills it intends the House to deal with. It is assumed that this speech will determine the main bulk of the legislative work of parliament for the year.

But now let us look at the other extreme, at the Congress of the United States. Who decides what Bills it will deal with? The answer cannot be stated positively with any great precision. It is true that the executive will have suggestions to make, and that in presidential messages the Congress will be urged to pass Bills on particular subjects. But that is as far as it goes. It is tempting to go to the other extreme and say that it is the legislature itself which decides what it will deal with. But this is too simple. The legislature as a whole does not decide it. It is decided by a group of leaders of the legislature, organized for the most part into a committee or committees for the purposes of arranging the business of Congress. The leaders of the majority party will have a great say in this, and, particularly in the House of Representatives, the Speaker of that House who, unlike the politically neutral Speaker of the British House of Commons, is the leader of the majority party. Seniority will have determined, to a large extent, who these leaders are. Here, too, as in Britain, there will be some Bills like money Bills, which will have to be dealt with. And there will be pressure on the congressional leaders, both from the administration and from other interested parties, to persuade them to bring forward certain Bills, which means that they are not completely free to do as they please.

In a way there is a striking resemblance between the British and the American way of dealing with Bills. In both cases it is the leaders of the legislature who settle what the legislature will deal with. But the difference is—and it makes all the difference—that the leaders of the legislature in Britain are the government, whereas in the United States they are separated from the government. Yet we cannot leave the whole matter there, with the implication that under the cabinet system the government is in charge and under the presidential system the leaders of the legislature are in charge. For in this matter of law making, as in so many others, cabinet systems differ. In many European legislatures for example, the answer to our question is almost the same as it is in the United States. It is not the government which decides what Bills the legislature shall deal with, nor the legislature itself, but a group of people in authority in the legislature. The group contains as a rule the presiding officer of the assembly and his deputies, the chairmen of the committees into which these assemblies are accustomed to divide themselves for the discussion of Bills, and, sometimes, the chairmen of the principal political parties or groups in the Assembly. The government's wishes are given consideration but they do not necessarily prevail. Making the laws is thought of as pre-eminently the assemblies' own business and they feel entitled through their own steering or co-ordinating machinery to decide what Bills they will deal with. France, under the Third and Fourth Republics, provided an extreme example of this system, but under the Fifth Republic, the government's position has been considerably strengthened, and its predominance in deciding what Bills shall be dealt with comes close to that of the British cabinet. The agenda of the two houses must give priority to government Bills and in the order which the government determines. One result has been a large drop in the number of private members' Bills laid before the assembly—at the end of the Fourth Republic there was an annual average of 2,200 private members' Bills; in the first parliamentary year of the Fifth Republic the number was about one-tenth of this figure.

4

A similar pattern of difference between legislatures is found throughout the whole process of law making. It is illustrated when we proceed to answer some further questions. Let us ask now: Whose Bills does the legislature deal with? The answer in Britain is: The government's Bills, except in so far as the government allows some time—and nowadays it allows a little—for Bills introduced by private members. On an average, and allowing for variations from year to year, about 85 per cent. of Bills presented in the British parliament since 1945 were government Bills, and about 15 per cent. were private members' Bills. But the main task is dealing with the government's Bills, which come straight to the House, prepared by the government, and the House is then called upon to give them a second reading. After that, though amendments may be proposed and even accepted at the committee stage, it is still the government's Bill, the principles of which, as accepted at the second reading, must stand.

Moreover in financial matters private members have no initiative. By Standing Orders no proposal for the raising or spending of money may be put forward in the British House of Commons except with the approval of the Crown, that is to say of the government; though a private member may propose a decrease in the amount of money to be spent, he cannot propose an increase. Thus in the most important sphere of legislation, the government retains complete initiative; all financial legislation is government legislation, and its consideration occupies the major part of the time of the House of Commons.

In most Commonwealth countries, and in Ireland and South Africa there is a similar allocation of time between government Bills and private members' Bills. Initiative in financial legislation is restricted to the government, not by standing orders, but by the constitutions of these countries. In non-financial spheres private members have an opportunity to introduce Bills, but only a small part of the time of the legislature is devoted to dealing with them. Many of the Bills introduced and passed are not of negligible importance —it is worth recalling that compulsory voting in elections to the two houses of the Australian parliament was established by an Act introduced by a private member. But many Bills are introduced with no hope that they will become law. The major part of the time of Commonwealth legislatures is taken up with the discussion of government Bills.

In the United States the position is different, technically because all Bills are private members' Bills since no member of the government may sit in Congress, and actually because of the greater part played in the drafting and discussion of Bills by Congressmen and Senators. It is true that suggestions for major measures of legislation come from the President and the departments, and that the financial messages of the president and the financial requirements of the departments form the raw material upon which Congress works in

deciding upon its appropriation and taxing acts. It
has been calculated that half of the Bills introduced
originate with the administration. But the committees
of both houses and both houses themselves regard
themselves as free to modify the administration's proposals as they think fit. And there is no rule to prohibit
Congressmen and Senators from introducing measures
which would result in the spending of money or in the
imposition of taxes. The result is that a very large
number of Bills is introduced each year—a rough
estimate puts the figure at 7,000 on an average. Very
many of these are trivial; very many receive little or no
attention from either house. But of those that do receive
serious consideration, those Bills introduced on the
initiative or in response to the urgings of the President
or the administration might well be in the minority.
And what is true of the Congress at Washington is true,
generally speaking, of the state legislatures also.

In European legislatures the practice is usually
nearer to that of Britain and other Commonwealth
countries than it is to the United States. The Fifth
French Republic has adopted in its constitution the
rule of the British House of Commons preventing
private members from taking the initiative in financial
legislation. It is provided that private members' Bills
or amendments by members are out of order if they
would have as a consequence either the diminution of
public revenue or the creation or increase of public
expenditure. It is as a result of this rule as much as of
the rule that government Bills have priority in the
houses over other Bills, that the initiative of the private
member in the French legislature has declined considerably under the Fifth Republic from what it was in

the Third and Fourth. In this matter France, for the time being at least, comes close to the British practice.

In Sweden the initiative of private members is freely exercised, and their proposals receive serious consideration by the chambers and their committees. They are not as important in subject matter as the proposals of the government, but they usually outnumber them. The number of government Bills varies between 200 and 250 a year; the proposals of private members have exceeded 700 in one year, and 500 a year would be normal. Sweden appears to be exceptional, among European legislatures, in giving such scope to the initiative of private members. In the Netherlands it appears to be used sparingly, and the greater part of the annual legislation is produced by the government. The explanation here, and in other European legislatures may be found not in the government's dominance over the legislature (as in Britain), but in the willingness of the government to introduce measures which satisfy the aspirations of private members. The give and take between legislature and government, combined perhaps with the smaller size of the legislatures, ensures that the wishes of even a small body of legislators will be acceded to by the government. What truth there is in an explanation of this kind is difficult to say.

The really important distinction between legislatures, however, when we come to answer the question: 'Whose Bills are dealt with?' does not rest upon statistics and proportions of government Bills and private members' Bills, interesting as these may be. It is the distinction between those legislatures in which Bills are dealt with first in the whole assembly itself and unless and until approved there, go no further; and those legislatures in which Bills go straight to a committee of the legislature, and thereafter come for consideration to the whole assembly itself. Roughly speaking, then, the answer, in these latter legislatures, to the question: 'Whose Bills are dealt with?' is 'The Bills produced from and by the standing committees of the legislature.' They may have been initiated by the government; they may be the work of private members; they may have been thought up by the standing committee itself; but whatever the process, until they have passed through the committee, they do not reach the legislature as a whole. This gives great power to the committees to modify, delay, ignore, or even kill a Bill, subject, however, as a rule, to the power of the assembly itself to require the committees to submit a report on the Bill to the whole house, though this power naturally is used exceptionally. There is a deep distinction here between law making in Britain and in Commonwealth countries on the one hand, where the legislature is invited right at the start to accept or reject the principles of the Bill before it goes to committee, and the United States and European countries where the legislature is not asked for its views until the committee has itself decided not only the details but also the principles of the Bill.

The freedom or licence with which committees of the legislature treated government Bills under the Third and Fourth French Republics led to some restrictions being inserted in the Constitution of the Fifth Republic. It was laid down that the text which the assembly would deal with, in the case of a government Bill, would be the government's text, not the text produced after discussion and amendment in the committee. So also when the Bill passed to the upper chamber, the discussion was to be upon the text agreed upon in the first chamber. Moreover, the government is placed in a stronger position in relation to amendments. No amendment which has not been previously considered by the committee will be considered in the chamber if the government objects. The government may also require the assembly by a single vote to reject all the amendments to the whole or a part of a Bill, except those proposed or accepted by the government. The power of the assembly to massacre government Bills, which was so notorious a feature of the Third and Fourth Republics, is thus considerably restricted. The position in France under the Fifth Republic is much nearer to that in Britain.

5

Let us ask the next and fourth question: Who is in charge of Bills in the legislature? In Britain, in Commonwealth countries, and in Ireland, and South Africa, if we ignore private members' Bills which are in the charge of their sponsors, the government, or rather the minister concerned, is in charge of a Bill throughout its stages. In the United States, on the other hand, it is the chairman of the committee concerned who is in charge of a Bill, aided by its sponsor or by other congressional leaders. In European legislatures as a rule it is the chairman or the *rapporteur* or some similar spokesman of the committee who is in charge of the Bill, even of government Bills. An extreme position is adopted in Sweden where, when a Bill is being considered in committee, ministers are not permitted to be present. The legislature has its own machinery and institutions for the direction and control of the making of laws. No better symbol of this function can be found than the two rows of seats—to refer once more to the symbolism of furniture—reserved in the French National Assembly for chairmen of committees and *rapporteurs,* and placed alongside and immediately to the left of the two rows reserved for ministers. And we will remember that, in the Third and Fourth Republics, at least, while the occupants of the two rows reserved for ministers changed frequently, the chairmen did not. Ministers might come and go; they remained. In the Fifth Republic, ministers are in charge of government Bills and, as already described, may move their own amendments and seek the rejection in a single vote of all those they dislike.

6

There is a further question which may seem rather technical but is indeed of great practical importance. Who decides the order in which Bills will be considered in the legislature? If a government has a programme and an order of priorities, it matters a great deal that measures shall be considered in the right order. Consequently, it is not surprising to learn that in Britain and in Commonwealth countries it is the government which decides the order in which Bills will be taken, and what is more that government business has priority over other business. It is true that the government consults the opposition before it announces the order of business. Where Bills are concerned, however, it is the government's duty and right to say just in what order it wishes its measures to be discussed. The party leaders in the legislatures of the

United States determine these matters. The presidents
of the chambers, the presidents of the committees and
the presidents or leaders of political parties or groups
in European legislatures—with the Fifth French
Republic as an exception—consider these questions
and they draw up time-tables which the legislature
usually accepts. The government may not like them; it
may use its influence to get them changed, but it has
no overriding authority in deciding the order of
business.

7

Closely connected with a time-table, if not actually
part of it, are arrangements for bringing discussions to
an end—for closures and guillotines and adjournments.
This brings us to the sixth question: Who decides how
long a legislature is to take in dealing with a Bill?
This is a difficult question to answer simply, for it
involves generalizing briefly about a complicated
matter. The rules about the curtailment of debate are
rather involved. And so they should be; for they are
concerned with a fundamental principle in the organization of legislatures, namely freedom of speech. If the
gag may be easily applied by majorities we come soon
to a dictatorship which is none the better because it is
imposed by an elected majority. Legislatures have had
to be very careful, therefore, to surround provisions for
closure with strict safeguards. Some legislatures indeed
have no closure provision at all. Sweden is an example.
In others as in Holland, Denmark, Norway, and Belgium, the power to move a closure motion is restricted
to the presiding officer or to a given number of members. It is in fact little used. In some cases, like the

American Senate, the conditions to be fulfilled for a closure to be effective are so formidable that the provision is almost a dead letter. It requires the signatures of at least sixteen Senators to initiate a closure; thereafter forty-eight hours must elapse before a vote upon whether or not to adopt a closure is permitted; to carry the motion for a closure requires a two-thirds majority of those present and voting; and if the motion is carried a possible 100 hours of debate can occur—one hour for each Senator. As a result the closure is very seldom applied. In contrast the House of Representatives in the United States restricts debate by a number of devices and a filibuster, a frequent feature of the Senate's history, is practically unknown in the House.

It is clear that in most legislatures, the danger of a tyranny of the majority is appreciated. When we consider the position in Britain we find that another principle is recognized also. The tyranny of the majority is one thing; but what about the tyranny of the minority? Is there not a danger that minorities by prolonged eloquence, may frustrate the government and bring business to a standstill? Is this a desirable way to behave? The result is that in Britain the procedure about closures boils down to this: provided the minority, the opposition, has been given a fair opportunity to have its say, the government is entitled to have its way. Minorities may oppose, but they must not obstruct; and majorities must not suppress, but they are entitled to win. Thus, by a number of procedures, some of which require the Speaker's consent, others the consent of a certain number of members, and so on, the rules of the House of Commons about how long the legislature may take over Bills work out so that the government can get a decision on its measures.

After the history of obstruction in the Third and Fourth Republics, the framers of the Constitution of the Fifth Republic looked for a means of forcing a decision upon the parliament. The provisions, already described, by which the government can raise the question of confidence upon a Bill achieve this object. The Bill is regarded as passed unless within twenty-four hours a motion of censure is put down and carried in accordance with the rules, namely that a majority of the whole assembly shall vote in favour of it. The budget of 1960 was indeed carried in this way, from the failure of a vote of censure. In the matter of the budget, indeed, the government has special powers to overcome obstruction. If the Assembly has not concluded its deliberation of the budget Bill with a decision within forty days, the Bill goes to the Senate, which must come to a decision within fourteen days. If thereafter, the two houses have not agreed within seventy days from the first introduction of the Bill, the government can put the Bill into operation by ordinances.

In American and European legislatures, however—speaking very generally and treating the Fifth French Republic as an exception—the emphasis is more upon the right of the minorities to criticize and oppose and obstruct than it is upon the right of the government to win. When closures are applied, too, they will usually be at the instance and under the control of the leaders in the legislature rather than of the government. This is true not only in the United States where the government is not in the legislature, but in European cabinet systems too. In this matter of controlling the time of the

legislatures we find one more illustration of the difference in strength between European cabinets, on the
one hand and the British Cabinet on the other. The
danger in the American and European systems is
the danger of obstruction and nullity; the danger in
Britain is the danger of turning the House of Commons
into a machine for registering front bench decisions for
or against a Bill; where what is said in the House is far
less important than what is done in the division
lobbies.

8

There is one further question, of a practical kind:
Whose Bills get passed in these legislatures? After all
that has been said about the government's control in
Britain of the initiation of Bills and of their passage
through parliament, it is not surprising to find that the
great majority of the Bills passed by parliament in
Britain are government Bills, and that almost all of the
Bills which the government introduces are passed. It is
very rare for a government Bill to be defeated: some
Bills are dropped for lack of time or enthusiasm as the
session comes to an end.

To make a comparison with what happens in the
United States is hardly possible, for all Bills introduced
in Congress are, technically at least, not government
Bills but private members' Bills. What is more, where
there is no restriction upon the introduction of Bills,
such as that provided in Britain over private members'
Bills by the government, the number of Bills introduced
is very great, and the proportion of those passed to
those introduced is low. Out of the 7,000 or so Bills
introduced on an average each year into the American

Congress nowadays fewer than 500 are passed. Of those passed, some are major Bills and many quite trivial. Some notion of the influence which the administration had in the making of laws in the United States may be obtained from figures which Lawrence H. Chamberlain published in 1946. He took ninety major Acts of Congress passed in the previous half-century and concluded that 20 per cent. of them were mainly prepared by the government, 30 per cent. were joint products of presidential and congressional influence, 40 per cent. were chiefly the product of Congress itself and less than 10 per cent. were the work of outside groups.

In the Fourth French Republic many more Bills were introduced than in Britain—about 1,400 a year as against 80 a year. So also the proportion of those passed was lower—in France an average of 275 were passed, in Britain an average of 70. And while in Britain 95 per cent. of the bills passed were introduced by the government, in France it was only 60 per cent.

Statistics of this kind are not of much use beyond a certain point, for they do not distinguish the important Bills from the trivial, nor do they measure the effort required in getting Bills passed or indicate the amount of compromise which governments may have had to make in getting Bills through nor do they take account of the fact that several members may table Bills on the same subject and these Bills may all contribute to the law eventually passed. What they may help to illustrate is the very different position in which representative assemblies stand so far as making the laws is concerned. Speaking generally, there is a great division between systems like the British where one might say

that the government makes the laws with the advice
and consent of the representative assembly and
systems like the American or the European where the
representative assembly makes the laws with the advice
and consent of the government. And, one may add, not
always with the consent of the government, for in the
United States, for example, though the President has a
veto over Bills passed by Congress and uses it regularly,
Congress may override his veto by re-passing the Bill
with a two-thirds majority in each House—and it does
this from time to time, and on quite important Bills.[1]
So potentially Congress in the United States makes the
laws whether the government likes them or not.

It is well known that, in many countries, law making
by the legislature is only a part of the law making that
goes on. In particular the practice has grown up by
which the legislature delegates a rule-making power to
the government or to independent or quasi-indepen-
dent administrative agencies. Whether this should be
described as a delegation of the law-making power or
not is a matter of discussion in some countries. Under
the Constitution of the United States it would seem
that Congress cannot delegate the law-making power.
But some rule-making power is needed by modern
governments and in the United States there is no doubt
at all that it is exercised. A glance at the *Code of Federal
Regulations* or at a volume of *The Federal Register*

[1] The President has ten days in which to decide whether
or not to veto a Bill. If Congress adjourns before the expiry
of the ten days and the President vetoes a Bill, that veto is
final and cannot be overriden. This is called the 'pocket veto'
and may be used only on the mass of Bills passed at the end
of a session of Congress.

illustrates the extent of the delegated powers of rule making. It has been left to the Supreme Court to say whether, in a particular case, an Act of Congress delegating a rule-making power to the administration went so far in the unlimited width of the powers it handed over, that it could be said to be delegating the law-making power. In 1935 the court in two cases which came before it did invalidate certain legislation on this ground, but it had not done so before nor has it done so since. The notion of subordinate regulations, of subordinate legislation, is accepted by the Supreme Court as consistent with the Constitution.

In Britain no question can arise in a court as to whether the power to delegate legislative authority is valid or not. There is no doubt that parliament may delegate such powers as it wishes to the government. The only question which can arise in a court is as to the extent of the powers delegated—a question of interpreting the meaning of the Act of Parliament. In Britain, as in the United States, a very large part of the law is made under delegated powers by the administration. The sheer bulk of delegated legislation in Britain overshadows legislation by parliament itself.

The Constitution of the Fourth French Republic said that the National Assembly alone had the right to legislate and that it could not delegate this right. None the less the power to legislate by decree was granted to the executive from time to time by the legislature. The position is regularized by the Constitution of the Fifth Republic where, in addition to the government's own powers to make laws under the Constitution, it is provided that the parliament may authorize the government to make ordinances, during a limited period, upon matters which are normally within the parliament's own legislative power.

It is not appropriate here to go into details in discussing the problems of making and controlling delegated legislation. We are concerned primarily with the position of legislatures in relation to delegated legislation, and we can best consider the question by asking: How far do legislatures control the exercise of powers of delegated legislation? And here, as elsewhere, it is found that their practices differ.

In Britain, we have what is almost an extreme case. It is the regular practice to require parliamentary approval for the exercise of powers of delegated legislation. Statutory instruments, as they are called, are made subject to the rule that they are void if parliament annuls them by a resolution within a specified period— usually forty days; or, less frequently, they go into effect only upon the passing of an affirmative resolution by parliament. Although not all statutory instruments are laid before parliament in this way, it is safe to say that most important instruments are so laid. Moreover, both houses of the British parliament have appointed select committees to scrutinize delegated legislation and to draw the attention of the house to what is considered unsatisfactory in their form or purport.

The House of Lords has had such a committee since 1925, the House of Commons since 1944. A similar procedure has been adopted in some other Commonwealth countries. The Australian Senate established a regulations and ordinances committee in 1937, and the Indian House of the People a committee on subordinate legislation in 1953.

Other legislatures do not go anything like so far as the British in requiring parliamentary approval of delegated legislation. It is rare for the American Congress to require it—an important example is the requirement that schemes of governmental reorganization drawn up by the President must, under the Reorganization Acts of 1939 and later, be laid before Congress for approval. Generally speaking, however, the safeguards sought in the United States are those of careful drafting in the acts which delegate rule-making powers, hearings of interested parties through administrative procedures before rules are promulgated, and the control of the courts of law whose sphere of intervention under the Constitution is considerably wider than in Britain or indeed in most other countries.

In European countries, some legislatures have little to do with the control of delegated legislation. This appears to be the position in Denmark and Norway, and to a large extent in the Netherlands, though in this last country it is not unusual for a statute to require that rules made under it shall lapse unless confirmed by an act of the legislature. In Belgium and in Ireland, however, delegated legislation usually needs parliamentary approval. In the Fifth Republic the ordinances made by the government under powers delegated for a limited period by the parliament, though they come into force on publication, cease to have effect if they are not submitted to the parliament for ratification before the date fixed in the Act which granted the ordinance-making power. Here, obviously, all depends upon the limits of time placed in the Act by the parliament.

What control amounts to in practice is hard to say.

In American and European legislatures, the government is so closely controlled and criticized by committees of the legislature that tyranny through the exercise of powers of delegated legislation cannot easily be accomplished. Nor will legislatures, as a general rule, be ready to delegate wide powers at the mere request of the government. In Britain, where the legislature formally has extensive powers of control, the strength of the cabinet in the legislative process generally modifies the opportunities and the effectiveness of criticism.

9

We may return, in conclusion, to the distinction, mentioned at the beginning of this chapter, between parliaments and legislatures. In both types of assembly it is accepted that there must be some sort of organization for making the laws. It cannot just be left to a large public meeting. The principle which John Stuart Mill laid down over a hundred years ago in his *Representative Government* is applied in almost all these modern assemblies. He wrote: 'A numerous assembly is as little fitted for the direct business of legislation as for that of administration.' But where they differ is in the organization which they devise for making the laws and in the relation of this organization to the government. While in Britain and most Commonwealth countries it is the government which has the predominant responsibility for organizing the legislative process, elsewhere responsibility is organized differently. There is, if not a body of leaders of the legislature, at least of managers of it, who may co-operate with the government or may not, and may include ministers or may not, but are, in any case, a distinct institution of the legislature with a responsibility to it. These assemblies also organize themselves into specialized committees, each of which deals with bills which fall within its competence, and it is regarded as obviously part of a committee's function to prepare a bill. Each member of these assemblies is, therefore, entitled to think of himself as a legislator. Each American Congressman, for example, may reasonably aspire to deserve the epitaph upon his law-making activities for which the Hon. Elijah Pogram asked in *Martin Chuzzlewit*: 'He was a member of the Congress of our common country, and was active in his trust.'

In law making they are very active. It is interesting to contrast the proceedings in a standing committee of the British House of Commons debating a Bill with what happens in the committees of foreign legislatures as they prepare a Bill. It is rare indeed in a British standing committee for the government's back bench supporters to speak at all. They leave it to the minister to deal with the criticisms and amendments which the opposition is putting forward. But in foreign committees all members, and particularly the members of the larger or majority parties, are active. As part of the process in some countries—the United States or Sweden, for example—committees hear evidence from witnesses, public hearings may be held, prolonged discussions go on, while the text of the Bill is gradually framed for submission to the legislature. They are indeed making the laws.

Such assemblies, then, may properly claim the title of legislatures, though they perform other functions as

well. On the other side are the assemblies we call parliaments—assemblies whose principal business is talk.
We are familiar with the criticism of parliaments, that
they do nothing but talk. 'There has seldom been
more misplaced derision', said John Stuart Mill, and
he went on in words which carry conviction:

I know not how a representative assembly can more use-
fully employ itself than in talk, when the subject of talk
is the great public interests of the country, and every
sentence of it represents the opinion either of some
important body of persons in the nation, or of an
individual in whom some such body have reposed their
confidence.

For Mill the proper function of a representative
assembly was to be a congress of opinions, a grand
inquest of the nation, a place for talking, not a place for
doing. Laws should not be made without its consent,
and the price which the government must pay for consent was to listen to the advice of the assembly. What
Mill advocated a century ago is still substantially the
doctrine of today. Making the laws in Britain is something for which the government is responsible; in most
foreign countries where democratic institutions exist,
it is something for which the representative assemblies
are responsible.

What, then, are we to think of these two very
different systems of making the laws? Each in its way
is in danger of going to an extreme. In the American
system there is the extreme of too many leaders and too
little leadership, an extreme notoriously illustrated also
by the Third and Fourth French Republics; in the
British there is the extreme of too much leadership;

overleadership, 'overlordship' if you like—what a critic like Ramsay Muir called 'the all but irresponsible autocracy of the Cabinet', and what others call 'cabinet dictatorship'. This type of phrase is not, one may suggest, a true description of the law-making process in Britain. It ignores or fails to recognize sufficiently the fact that although the government seldom loses a Bill, it seldom introduces a Bill it would be likely to lose. British governments are responsive as well as responsible. It does, however, draw attention in an exaggerated way to the fact that so few back benchers, and particularly on the government side, have any significant share in the actual making of laws, in comparison with members of representative assemblies in America and in European countries.

The opinions which clerks of the British House of Commons have expressed on this point deserve careful consideration. These experienced officials, though spectators and not participants in the parliamentary game, like all spectators see, if not most of the game, at least parts of it which the players may not see so well. And before two select committees of inquiry into the procedure of the House, in 1930 and 1946, the clerks suggested ways in which ordinary members might be better able to take a hand in the work of the House. It is interesting that on each occasion they suggested the use of specialized committees, each allotted a sphere of policy in which to operate. In this way members would get an opportunity to know more about proposed legislation and the background of administration from which it originated. But such suggestions have usually been rejected on the ground that they would lead the British parliament straight into the extreme of ministerial instability which was found in France.

But the alternative to the British system of the dominant stable executive as was suggested earlier is not necessarily or initially the weak unstable executive of the Third and Fourth Republics; there is a middle way of moderate stability which the Low Countries and Scandinavia illustrate. Neither British front bench, however, seems interested in this middle way; neither ministers in office nor potential ministers in opposition wish the powers of the government to be reduced.

Chapter Seven

MAKING PEACE AND WAR

I

FIRST a word about terms. By 'making peace' is meant something more than the mere formalities of making a treaty of peace; it is intended to include the whole process of conducting diplomatic relations between states, the process by which peace is organized and maintained and international relations are conducted. Similarly 'making war' includes not only the formal declaration of war, but the whole process of preparing for war, waging war when war is once declared and winding up after a war. In other words, we are thinking of foreign affairs and defence. These are very big subjects. Our interest in them is strictly limited. The question that concerns us is how far legislatures have influence and authority in the making of peace and war as so defined. And we shall deal separately with the two topics, taking the making of peace first.

Generally speaking it is the practice in most countries that the mouthpiece through which a country speaks to another country is the executive. Where important differences occur is in the part which legislatures play in determining what the executive may or shall say. In trying to analyse the position it is essential to pay attention not only to the formal or legal powers of executive and legislature in this matter, but also to their powers in practice and in day-to-day operation.

2

The United States and the United Kingdom illustrate two almost extreme positions in their arrangements for conducting foreign relations. To understand their different systems it is worth while to make use of a rough distinction between the process of forming obligations and the process of performing the obligations once they have been formed. Up to a point this is the distinction between undertaking obligations which are binding in international law and giving these obligations binding force in municipal or national law. In the United Kingdom, it is competent, so far as the law is concerned, for the Crown, that is to say for the Queen on the advice of her ministers, to conclude a treaty with a foreign state. The whole process of negotiation, signature and ratification lies within the legal powers of the executive: participation by the legislature is not required. In the forming of obligations, that is to say, the legislature need have no part. In the United States, on the other hand, no treaty can be made unless it receives the approval of two-thirds of the Senate; that is of the Senators present on the occasion. It is interesting to notice that it is the approval not of the whole legislature but of a part only of it which is required. Thus the American executive may speak to foreign states, and is indeed the official mouthpiece of the United States, but it cannot bind the country in a treaty without the consent of the Senate.

When we come to consider the performing of obligations, similar important differences show themselves. In the United States, treaties become part of the law of the United States by the very same process as that by which they are ratified. The Constitution says: 'All treaties made, or which shall be made, under the authority of the United States, shall be the supreme law of the land; and the judges in every state shall be bound thereby, anything in the constitution or laws of any state to the contrary notwithstanding.' This means that in the United States treaties are made part of the municipal law of the United States at the same time as the United States assumes obligations in international law. What is more, it follows from the wording of the Constitution that if a treaty conflicts with an earlier Act of Congress (though not with the Constitution itself, which is superior to all other legal instruments) it prevails over that earlier Act to the extent to which it conflicts with it. On the other hand a later Act of Congress could alter or reject the provisions of a treaty. State legislatures, however, are without power to alter treaty provisions.

In the United Kingdom the question of performing treaty obligations is determined according to the subject matter of the treaty. Put shortly the position is that if a treaty, to be effective, requires the law of the land to be altered, that alteration can be made only by the authority of an Act of Parliament—the consent of the legislature must be obtained. Thus a treaty which altered customs duties, or which imposed some other charge upon the people, could not become effective in British law unless the alterations were made by, or under the authority of an Act of Parliament. As a result it is usual nowadays for treaties of this kind not to be ratified until parliament has passed the necessary legislation or for the signature or ratification of such a treaty to be carried out subject to the consent of parliament. On the other hand, a treaty of alliance, for example, can be concluded by the executive and is regarded as of full legal force within the country without the passage of legislation by parliament.

When we look at the practice in some other countries we find certain variations upon the procedure which applies in the United States and the United Kingdom. Commonwealth countries usually adopt the legal provisions which apply in the United Kingdom—though in practice, as we shall see, their exercise of the legal powers sometimes differs from the British. The provisions of the Constitution of the Fifth French Republic have a similarity, on paper at least, to the position in Britain, though the area in which the consent of the legislature is required is probably greater. The President of the Republic negotiates and ratifies treaties—a change from the Fourth Republic where he merely signed and ratified treaties, and was to be kept informed of international negotiations. In the Fifth Republic the President is to be kept informed of all negotiations leading to the conclusion of an international agreement not subject to ratification. But although the President may negotiate treaties, he requires the counter signature of the Prime Minister and the minister of foreign affairs to his actions in signing treaties, and his powers of ratification are circumscribed by the right of the legislature in most important areas. Peace treaties, commercial treaties, treaties or agreements relative to international organization, those which involve the finances of the state, those which modify provisions of a legislative nature, those which are relative to the status of persons, those which require cession, exchange or acquisition of territory, can be ratified or approved only by a law, and they take effect only after having been ratified and approved. Most of the matters mentioned here would, in Britain and in Commonwealth countries, require the action of the legislature to bring them into effect. It is interesting to notice also that the list is substantially the same as that which appeared in the Constitution of the Fourth Republic. So also is a provision that treaties or agreements which have been regularly ratified and approved, have, on their publication, a superior authority to that of the laws, but a new condition is added in the Fifth Republic, namely that the agreement or treaty is applied by the other party.

In most other European legislatures, while the executive negotiates and signs treaties, their ratification requires the approval of the legislature, and any obligations undertaken which involve changes in the legal rights of citizens or involve financial obligations require action by the legislature.

Switzerland takes the matter almost to an extreme. Not only is the consent of the legislature required for the carrying of treaties into effect but 'treaties with foreign powers concluded for an undetermined period or for more than fifteen years shall be submitted to the people for acceptance or rejection on the demand of 30,000 Swiss citizens entitled to vote, or of eight cantons'. The referendum thus has a place in the performance of certain treaties in Switzerland, but it is to be noted that the reference to the people is not obligatory; it requires initiative on the part of those who object to what has been negotiated. In practice these

provisions of the Constitution, which were first introduced into it in 1921, have been used only once since
that time, although, up to 1952, twenty-two treaties
fell within the challengeable class. On the one occasion,
however, the people at the referendum rejected the
treaty submitted to them. This occurred in 1923, when
a convention concluded between Switzerland and
France concerning the *zones franches* around Geneva
was refused approval decisively.

3

What has been said so far concerns very largely the
letter of the law concerning treaties. If we are to
understand the subject at all, however, we must consider the matter more widely. To begin with, the making and implementing of treaties is quite a small part
of conducting foreign affairs. Treaties and other such
formal conventions are indeed comparatively rare in
international relations. There are other and less formal
ways of making agreements and arrangements between
states. And in this respect the United States provides
some most interesting material in the development of
the use of the 'executive agreement' as it has come to be
called. If the President of the United States wishes to
conclude some arrangement with a foreign state he is
not bound to make it in the form of a treaty, with the
consequent necessity of obtaining for it the consent of
two-thirds of the Senate. He may simply make an
agreement on his own authority and sign it. Thereby
he commits the United States. It was decided in 1937
by the Supreme Court of the United States, in the case
of *United States* v. *Belmont* that such an executive
agreement had the same legal effect as a treaty duly

made and ratified. Of course an executive agreement might be abrogated by a later President and for this reason foreign countries might prefer a treaty which had received the approval of the Senate. But there might indeed, on balance, be little to choose between the security afforded by either type of agreement, and executive agreements as a rule could be concluded more speedily and with less public controversy.

It is clear that the use of the executive agreement reduces the influence of the legislature—or rather of the Senate—in the conduct of foreign relations in the United States. It is possible for Presidents to commit the United States and present legislatures with *faits accomplis* which they are in practice powerless to alter or reject. And by the ruling of the Supreme Court a President in so acting has both formed and performed the obligations contained in the agreement; he has produced an instrument which has force of law both internationally and nationally.

This is no theoretical possibility. The executive agreement is now commonly used in the conduct of American foreign relations. In recent years there have been some famous or notorious arrangements made by this means—President Franklin D. Roosevelt's exchange of destroyers with Britain in 1940 for bases in the Western Atlantic; his various agreements at Teheran and Yalta; and the similar arrangements made by President Truman at Potsdam. In earlier years President Theodore Roosevelt had arranged, by executive agreement with the Japanese government, the extent of Japanese immigration into the United States, an arrangement known as the Gentleman's Agreement which lasted for seventeen years until abrogated by Congress. And the 'Open Door Policy', which governed American policy in the Far East for a large part of this century, was similarly expressed in an executive agreement.

It is not surprising that this development should be criticized by those who prize the safeguard of the legislature's control over the executive. By the use of the executive agreement the American President achieves as free a hand as the British executive, in spite of the safeguards over the exercise of the treaty powers which are contained in the American Constitution. Indeed, in some ways, he has a freer hand, for what he concludes by executive agreement has force of law within the United States, whereas some agreements made by the British executive may well need to be accompanied by legislation before they become part of the law of the United Kingdom. It was against this development of the executive's power, with its consequent erosion of the Senate's control, that Senator Bricker, a Republican, of Ohio, devoted his attacks. He campaigned in 1953-4 to obtain an amendment of the Constitution of the United States, which would have restricted the treaty-making power and would have brought executive agreements under the control of Congress. He was indeed uneasy at the whole idea that a treaty once made, even if the Senate had approved it, should become the supreme law of the land. He felt that only Congress—that is House and Senate—should have the power to make such law. Executive agreements, he felt, were far worse for not even a part of the legislature had a say in approving them. Supporters of the Bricker Amendment, after much discussion and compromise, almost succeeded in 1954 in carrying in the Senate, at the end of a long campaign, a proposal for a constitutional amendment which would have made it necessary for an Act of Congress to be passed in order that an international agreement, other than a treaty, shall become effective as internal law in the United States. It is interesting to notice that this proposed amendment was sponsored by a Democrat, Senator Walter George of Georgia, and that it failed by only one vote to secure the two-thirds majority in the Senate necessary for a constitutional amendment to go forward.

It is a curious thing that, under the American system, where so much care was taken to associate at least a part of the legislature with the treaty-making procedure, there should have developed, by the use of the executive agreement, a situation where the legislature is less able to control the translation of international obligations into the law of the land than is possible in Britain or France, and many other countries in Europe and the Commonwealth. It is clear that in a sphere where the legislature may rightfully claim a place, namely the making of the law, the President, by the making of an executive agreement, makes the law, as a result of the decision of the Supreme Court in 1937.

The result should not be exaggerated, however, for when, in the United States, the President by executive agreement alters the law of the land, the legislature has the power always to revoke such an agreement by an Act, just as it can also amend or revoke any treaty to which the President and Senate have given consent. Thus an executive agreement in the United States can be revoked by Congress, though it must be remembered that any such revocation would need the consent of the

President, and if that were not forthcoming, a two-thirds majority would be needed in each house of Congress to override the veto. Where treaties are concerned, the House of Representatives finds itself at some disadvantage, for if the President and the Senate have agreed, then a treaty is of full effect as the law of the land, and any attempt by the House to revoke it might be expected to fail for lack of the Senate's consent.

To complete the picture of executive influence in these matters, it is proper to emphasize that foreign policy can be determined by many actions which fall far short of anything so formal as an executive agreement with a foreign state, much less a treaty. In the course of conducting discussions and negotiations with foreign states—a sphere in which, in almost all systems of government it is recognized that the executive has sole authority—policy is influenced inevitably. The executive gives assurances, encourages certain lines of action, condemns others, makes public announcements and speeches, or maintains silence at critical moments, recognizes governments or breaks off relations with them, sends congratulatory messages, calls or attends conferences or declines to do so, sends goodwill missions and receives them, and in a dozen other ways by open or secret methods, takes part in the formation of policy. In all or most of this the legislature has no part, although when it comes in due course to be consulted, its freedom of action has been limited by what the executive has done. How free the executive itself is in these matters depends, of course, upon the need there is for it to consult the legislature for final ratification of what is negotiated and upon the ease or difficulty with which the legislature's consent is usually obtained.

4

We have stressed so far the way in which the power of the executive has been developed, particularly in the United States, to the exclusion of the legislature from influence in the formation of foreign policy. This is a fairly general trend in all systems of government and is perhaps not unexpected. Throughout a period of prolonged international crisis, such as that which has occurred since 1914, and more particularly since 1939, it is inevitable that by reason of the urgency, the complication, the continuity and the secrecy of international negotiations, the executive should find itself obliged to take decisions and to conduct discussions without reference to the legislature. At the same time there have been developments in the other direction. Legislatures have extended their influence in some countries at least. Their relative position may still be unchanged or it may be weaker, because of the great increase in executive activity, but in absolute terms legislatures have made certain gains. It is worth while to notice some of these, in order that we may have a complete picture before us.

To begin with it is important to emphasize that when we speak of performing obligations, we should not think only of the narrow function of giving force of law within a state to the obligations undertaken by the state in international law. We should remember that the process of performing international obligations usually involves actions which require the consent of the legislature. The consequences of a treaty of alliance provide a good example. In Britain a treaty of alliance can be negotiated and ratified and become of full legal effect, internally as well as internationally, by the action of the Crown alone. The consent of parliament is not needed. But if that alliance requires or promises armed support to a country, as it usually does, the consent of parliament to the raising of the money to provide those armed forces is required. In the background of such a treaty, therefore, is the need for parliamentary support. Only a government which is able to secure parliamentary support in this way can confidently commit the country to such a treaty of alliance. Indirectly, and in the long run not less effectively, the legislature has a part to play in the performance, in the wider sense, of obligations which the executive alone has legal power to form and perform in the narrower sense.

And the same position is found in the United States. One of the interesting developments in the years since Franklin D. Roosevelt became President, has been the way in which the Congress—and not merely the Senate—has come to be associated with foreign affairs. The Senate, as has been explained, has always had a deciding voice where treaties are concerned, but the Senate is not the legislature. But in the United States, as in Britain, if American foreign policy is to be effective it must have armed support behind it, and in the voting of appropriations for defence in the United States it is the whole Congress whose consent is required, and it is the House of Representatives particularly which claims authority in those matters where taxation and appropriation are concerned.

But there have been other developments which have given to the legislature as a whole, and to the House of

Representatives in particular, a greater opportunity to be influential in foreign policy. The growth of American aid to foreign countries in Europe and Asia, as an important part of American foreign policy, which has been a leading feature of the administrations of President Franklin D. Roosevelt and his successors, has meant the passing of large appropriation Bills by the Congress. The consent of the House as well as of the Senate has been essential for the carrying out of these policies. The President may propose, but it is the legislature which can dispose. It is not too much to say, perhaps, that since 1945 the American policy of foreign aid has been a most important single factor in defence against the Soviet Union. The consent of the Congress has been necessary for the carrying out of this policy and its continuance must depend on that support. And the significance of this development is that the House of Representatives has thus come to play a greater part in foreign affairs.

There is another method by which a legislature can control foreign affairs. It can pass an Act restricting the action which the executive may take. Here again the United States supplies a good illustration. Congress passed Neutrality Acts in 1935 and later which were intended to keep the United States out of hostilities which might involve her in war. The President was authorized to place an embargo on the sale of arms to powers engaged in war, to restrict the movements of American ships and citizens in war zones, and to require those purchasing war materials to pay for them in cash and to carry them in non-American vessels. Although most of these requirements were not mandatory upon the President, the existence of the Act

showed strong support for a policy which he was
expected to treat with respect. And in fact President
Roosevelt did feel himself restricted by the legislation.
It was not until 1941 that it was repealed.

In Britain, while parliament has not noticeably
increased its power over foreign affairs through the
enactment of legislation, it has come to be more and
more important as a forum of debate. Discussions
upon foreign affairs since 1919 have been much more
frequent than before that period, and since 1945 they
are common. Though the Crown, through its ministers,
is reluctant to allow the legislature to tie its hand in
negotiations or to reveal beforehand the course of its
discussions with foreign powers, it feels obliged to
permit frequent debates and to justify itself before both
houses of parliament over a wide range of topics.
Foreign policy is no longer treated as a private preserve
of a minister—a department which parliament and the
public cannot discuss.

5

But there is lacking in the British parliament—and
in most of the Commonwealth parliaments also—an
institution which in the United States and in European
countries is an important instrument of the legislature's
influence in foreign affairs. That is the foreign affairs
or foreign relations committee. This is a particular
illustration of the difference in attitude towards the use
of committees in the British and Commonwealth
legislatures from that in other countries. The two
houses of Congress have their committees—foreign
relations in the Senate, foreign affairs in the House.
Foreign affairs committees are found in the legislatures

of European countries, and where these legislatures
have two chambers each chamber, as a rule, has its own
foreign affairs committee, with the exception of Sweden
where, like all Swedish standing committees, it is a
joint committee of members chosen in equal numbers
from the two houses. The committees vary in size and
in function. The foreign affairs committees of the
Chamber of Deputies under the Third French Republic and of the National Assembly under the Fourth
were composed of forty-four members, like other
standing committees, and they were very influential.
Leading members of the parties and groups sat on them
and they regarded themselves as entitled to a say over
the whole range of French foreign policy and its
administration. In the Fifth Republic the foreign affairs
committee of the Assembly has sixty members, and
its influence, though not negligible, has inevitably
declined while the predominant say in foreign policy
and its direction has rested with President de Gaulle.

The sixteen members of the Swedish foreign affairs
committee (eight from each house) act also as the
members of the Advisory Council on Foreign Affairs
which, meeting under the chairmanship of the King,
is the institution through which the government keeps
the legislature informed of developments in foreign
policy before decisions are taken. The foreign affairs
committee is the only standing committee of the
Swedish legislature which a minister is allowed to
attend—a necessary modification of the rule, if the
committee is to be adequately informed about the subject of its work. In the lower house of the legislature
of the Netherlands there is a very small committee
on foreign affairs of seven members which discusses

foreign policy with the minister of foreign affairs; there is a committee of the upper house also, but its functions are confined only to the asking of information from the minister and it is consequently less influential.

None of these committees engage in the public sittings which are such a feature of the two committees of the Congress of the United States. It is the regular practice of these latter committees to hear in public evidence from the administration, from other members of Congress and from almost all organizations or individuals who wish to give their views upon the foreign policy of the United States. Evidence is heard in private sessions also, but the public debate and controversy is a most important part of their activities and imposes special difficulties and burdens upon those charged with the task of conducting American relations with foreign countries. And, as has been mentioned already, the majority party in the committees on occasion can be the opposite party from that which provides the President and the administration. Yet a remarkable degree of bi-partisan co-operation has been achieved.

The Senate committee on foreign relations in the United States occupies a special position among committees on foreign relations, largely because of the special position which the Senate itself holds in the conduct of American foreign policy. Because no treaty may be ratified unless a majority of at least two-thirds of the Senators present votes in its favour, the opinions of the Senate's committees become very important and hearings before the committee in which arguments for and against a treaty may be advanced have considerable significance. A President and a secretary of state find it

wise to consult the chairman and at least the leading
members of the committee in the course of negotiations and may even associate them with the process.
A failure to consult has led to a refusal to ratify a
treaty when it came before the Senate. In fact the
Senate has agreed to the ratification of the great
majority of treaties that have been submitted to it, but
as among the exceptions was the Treaty of Versailles,
its power to reject a treaty is almost better known than
the measure of its agreement with the administration's
policy.

The Senate's committee obtains power in foreign
relations from one further prerogative which the Senate
itself possesses—the requirement that presidential
appointments to high office, and in this case, the
appointment of the secretary of state, of ambassadors
and other diplomatic officers need the approval of a
majority of the Senators present and voting. It is the
custom that the Senate's committee considers all
nominations to these appointments and makes recommendations to the Senate. Hearings are held, evidence
is presented for and against a nominee, he may be
questioned about his record, his views and his intentions. Although a nomination is seldom defeated, the
fact that a nominee must run the gauntlet of the Senate's committee is bound to limit the President's freedom to appoint whom he will to these offices in the
field of foreign relations.

In Britain and other Commonwealth countries the
setting up of foreign affairs committees in the legislature has been advocated from time to time. But the
strength of the division of the legislature into government and opposition in these countries has had a great

deal to do with the failure to establish these committees. Opposition parties are reluctant to join a committee with government supporters where, they fear, they will find themselves committed imperceptibly to government policy. They may be given information which they wish to use but are forbidden to use. They may hear of proposals or developments which they wish to denounce. They prefer to keep their freedom. When a foreign affairs committee was set up in the Australian House of Representatives in 1952, the opposition members refused to join it. Even where there is a good deal of agreement between the government and the opposition about foreign policy in Commonwealth countries, the opposition party or parties prefer to avoid co-operation through a committee of the legislature. Intra-party committees on foreign affairs are sometimes found and within the government party itself ministers may address private meetings either of such a committee or of the whole party to explain and defend the government's policies and to hear the views of their supporters. But apart from occasions of this kind, the rôle of the ordinary member of the legislature in Commonwealth countries so far as foreign affairs is concerned is largely confined to such opportunities as he gets in the debates—usually held at frequent intervals—in the whole house.

But a committee of the legislature is not the legislature itself. If the minister of foreign affairs is to be expected to speak frankly to a committee, he will do so only if he can be assured that what he says will not be divulged to the legislature as a whole. As a rule, therefore, in committees on foreign affairs, members are bound to secrecy, either about all that goes on in the committees, or about anything divulged to them by ministers which in the opinion of the ministers should be treated as secret. Reasons of secrecy, too, have led to objections being made to certain groups, such as the Communists, being represented on foreign affairs committees, and in the Netherlands since 1948 Communists have been excluded from the foreign affairs committee of the lower house. If they are present on such a committee of a legislature, inevitably the minister will feel unable to divulge confidential information about foreign policy, for fear that it will be disclosed to other states.

Complaints are frequently made that even if a minister speaks freely to a foreign affairs committee, the legislature as a whole is still left very much in the dark about what is going on or what is contemplated. What is called the 'democratic control of foreign policy' is not achieved through committees on foreign affairs. All that happens is that a few more people are taken into the government's confidence, and even they may not be taken very far. At the most it is a parliamentary oligarchy which is created, and this is not democracy. These criticisms are justified. Yet no minister of foreign affairs can ever be expected to tell the whole legislature of his country in public session or indeed in secret session anything which he is not prepared to tell the world. If foreign affairs are to be debated in public, ministers will wish to ensure that what is said in the debate and that the time at which it is said will reveal nothing detrimental to their country which can be of use to possible enemies. Legislatures as a whole can never be taken really into the confidence of foreign ministers to such an extent that they can be told what is secret and confidential. And though committees of the legislature may be given this confidence the use they can make of it is extremely limited. Whatever value there may be in the system of committees on foreign affairs in the legislature—and their work is highly valued in European legislatures—the fact remains that these committees are not the legislature.

The extent to which a legislature or a committee of a legislature can obtain knowledge and influence in foreign affairs depends in a great measure on the nature of a country's foreign policy. Where a country pursues a policy of neutrality, it would not be surprising if both the legislature and its committee were well informed about that country's foreign affairs. No doubt a policy of neutrality does not conduct itself automatically; a country may need to be very active to preserve its neutrality, and much of its activity may need to be secret. But the legislature will know what the policy is. To an outsider it would seem that the conduct of Swiss foreign policy could be carried out in association with the legislature to a very large extent. Swedish neutrality is no doubt a more complicated matter, but in both Switzerland and Sweden the association of the legislature with policy would seem to present less difficulty than arises in a country which pursues what might be called an 'active' foreign policy. If a country wishes to participate fully in international relations by using its influence and its power continuously, then the extent to which a legislature or even a committee of the legislature can be informed and consulted seems likely to be much less. They are bound to be behind the times; they are likely to be asked to approve *faits accomplis*;

they will seldom be afforded an opportunity for adequate prior consultation. Their control will tend to be confined to the broad outlines of policy and to the need for the executive to be sure that it can, in the last resort, count on the support of the legislature in what it has undertaken to do. For these reasons, at least, control by a legislature or a committee over foreign affairs may be more effective in one country than in another, and it would be unwise to conclude that what works in one country would, if transplanted, work as well in another.

6

We may turn now to the making of war and begin with the formal declaration of war. Here, so far as the letter of the law is concerned, countries fall roughly into two groups—those in which the executive alone has authority to declare war, and those where the consent of the legislature is necessary. The United Kingdom and most other Commonwealth countries are examples of the first class. The Crown declares war and there is no legal necessity for the consent of parliament. Sweden is in the same position. In the other group there are many countries. In the United States, under the Constitution, Congress alone has the power to declare war. The Constitution of the Fifth French Republic says that the declaration of war is authorized by the parliament. It is the general rule, indeed, in most European countries.

But here again we should not be misled by concentrating too closely upon the strictly legal position. In Britain, though the executive declares war, it will not do so unless it is convinced that it can obtain the support of the legislature. It is true that it can present it with a *fait accompli* and thereby almost compel it to support a war which the executive has started. On the other hand under the American system, though Congress alone can declare war, the President, as Commander-in-Chief of the armed forces of the United States can produce a situation where hostilities have occurred and in which it is almost impossible for Congress not to declare war. The shooting may have begun, though the war has not been declared. Under both systems the executive, through its control of the armed forces, can leave the legislature with little freedom of choice.

It is interesting to notice also that in some Commonwealth countries, where the law of the constitution is similar to that in Britain and where the executive alone can declare war, there is a strong constitutional convention that this should not be done without the consent of the legislature. Canada adopts this point of view, largely no doubt because of the differences of opinion on foreign affairs between French Canadians and English-speaking Canadians. Successive Canadian Prime Ministers have declared that Canada would not be involved in any war without the prior consent of the parliament. Such a course was followed in September 1939, when the Canadian Prime Minister called parliament together after the German invasion of Poland, and as a result of its approval, advised the King to declare war on Germany. The declaration was made on 10 September 1939, a week after the declaration by the government of the United Kingdom.

Since the conduct of war and the preparation for war involves considerable public expenditure, the imposition of compulsory military service, and the regulation by the state of almost every sphere of life, it is obvious that the legislature will be called upon to pass important laws to that end. While, therefore, the executive may declare war, it is clear that it needs the support of the legislature in preparing for war, and in prosecuting a war, and that it will be obliged to satisfy the criticisms of the legislature and obtain its consent to important decisions on policy.

The control which legislatures in various countries are able to exercise over policy and administration in defence follows a similar pattern to that already described in the field of foreign relations. In Britain and in other Commonwealth countries there are frequent debates in the legislature, some directly upon questions of policy, others arising out of debates upon financial legislation where the estimates and appropriations for defence departments come up for approval. In the British House of Commons, the estimates committee and the public accounts committee investigate the operation of the different defence departments and make reports from time to time about their proposed or past expenditure. But there are no specialized standing committees of the House on defence, any more than on foreign affairs or any other subject. Here again, if ministers are willing to speak privately to members they will do so to meetings of their own supporters.

In the Congress of the United States and in European legislatures specialized committees on defence are established, and committees on appropriations or on taxation will also feel entitled to investigate expenditure on defence. The American committees hold hearings on this subject as on others, and the heads of the different defence services, both serving officers and civilians, appear before them, and advocate, in public session and in private, the needs of their departments, very often in fierce competition with each other. Here again, as in foreign affairs, but even more so, the question of secrecy arises. There are strict limits upon what can be told in confidence to a committee, and there is nothing that can be told to the legislature as a whole which cannot be told to the whole world. Committees and legislatures may question and debate and protest; they may reduce or indeed (as has happened in the United States) increase the sums asked for by the administration; they can seldom be ignored. But over a wide area of the field of defence, as of foreign affairs, they are bound to be in the dark.

In times of war law making tends to become a function of the executive. It is usual for wide powers of rule making to be delegated to the executive by the legislature. The amount of emergency legislation produced by the executive in war-time far outweighs in bulk and, indeed, in importance, the laws made by the legislature itself. So also after a war, when efforts are being made to demobilize and to readjust the economy to peace-time conditions, emergency legislation by the executive usually continues. Such has been the experience after the First and Second World Wars in the United States, in Britain and in most Commonwealth and European countries. The great growth of delegated legislation in this century has come with and after the two world wars.

It is apparent that in making peace and in making war, executives tend to undertake functions which the legislature is likely to claim as its own. The extreme example is the exercise by the executive of the law-making power, whether by some such technique as the executive agreement in the United States or by the use of powers of delegated legislation as has happened in all countries in time of war. It is true, of course, that it is the legislature itself which delegates the law-making power and that the extent and the duration of these delegated powers is determined by the legislature. The ultimate control, therefore, in this matter is with the legislature. Moreover, it is usual to find that where the executive can legislate by making agreements with foreign states, the legislature has a power to amend or revoke the agreements by act if it wishes. Yet the necessities of international relations, the urgencies of crises, the rumours of wars, and the existence of war itself, forces the hand of the legislature and makes it inevitable that in these spheres the executive will gather power to itself. It is not too much to say that war, preparation for war, and the aftermath of war have, in this century, been important causes of that situation which some writers have described as 'the decline of legislatures'—a subject of which more will be said in our concluding chapter.

Chapter Eight

TWO CHAMBERS—MORE OR LESS?

I

MOST modern legislatures have two chambers. Even the revolutionary states, like the U.S.S.R., which claim to have broken with the bad old past, have a bicameral legislature, so that we find the Supreme Soviet composed of a Soviet of the Union and a Soviet of Nationalities. So strong is the urge towards bicameralism that the legislature in Norway, the 'Storting', which is elected as one body, breaks itself up into two parts, a 'Lagting' of thirty-eight members which is selected by the whole 'Storting', and an 'Odelsting' in which the remaining 112 members of the 'Storting' sit. On the other hand the states which have abolished their second chambers have not usually been in the category of the revolutionary. New Zealand, though a progressive country, is politically fairly sedate; under a Conservative government it abolished its second chamber in 1950. Denmark, in much the same category, did likewise in 1954. And it was radicalism rather than bolshevism which in 1922 led Queensland alone among the six states of Australia to abolish its second chamber and Nebraska in 1937 alone among the fifty States of the United States to do the same.

In speaking of 'second' chambers it is perhaps worth mentioning that there is some danger of misunderstanding because not all countries use the expressions 'first' and 'second' chambers in the same way. In

Britain or Canada or France or Italy, for example, the first chamber is the popularly elected assembly and the second chamber is the other one. In the United States or Australia where both chambers are popularly elected, it is the House of Representatives, composed in proportion to population, which is the first chamber, and the Senate, where each state is equally represented regardless of its population which is thought of as the second chamber. But in some countries—the Netherlands and Sweden are examples—the popularly elected Lower House is the second chamber; the indirectly elected Upper House is the first chamber. One way of avoiding misunderstanding in the use of 'first' and 'second' is to adopt the terms 'lower' and 'upper' chambers or houses and these will in fact be used from time to time in the course of the discussion that follows. But it seems permissible also to use 'first' and 'second' in the sense in which they are used by the majority of countries, while taking care, in the case of such countries as Sweden and the Netherlands, to make clear which chamber is being referred to by speaking of 'lower' and 'upper' houses.

2

It is not proposed to attempt in this chapter a detailed account of the composition and powers of the second chambers in all the countries whose legislatures have been discussed in preceding chapters. Instead one or two themes or issues will be raised and discussed in fairly general terms. And first of all, it may be worth while to try to get out of the way a doctrine about the proper function of a second chamber which seems to rest upon an illusion. It can be expressed in the words

which the mottled-faced gentleman in *Pickwick Papers*
addressed to Sam Weller: 'I object', he said, 'to the
introduction of politics.' Some people cherish the
notion of a second chamber above and beyond politics,
composed of eminent gentlemen and ladies, of great
distinction in various walks of life but politically
neuter. They might discuss political questions from
time to time but they would discuss them from an
independent and detached standpoint, unmoved, above
all, by party passions.

There is undoubtedly a case for saying that second
chambers should contain people who are less dependent
upon party considerations and party organizations than
are the members of lower houses. But if second chambers are to be anything more than debating societies or
discussion circles—and, if they are this, they will certainly not be valueless—party is bound to come in. If,
for example, second chambers are to have some powers
to discuss and vote on Bills, even if they are limited to
suggesting amendments or to imposing some short
delay upon the passage of a Bill, surely it will soon
become apparent whether the second chamber contains
a majority for the government or against it. One would
have thought that after twelve months' experience of
the working of a chamber of eminent persons it would
be possible to say with some certainty whether for
example it contained a Conservative majority or a
Labour majority.

There is really nothing surprising in this. The second
chamber is invited to give its opinion upon measures
and policies initiated and pushed forward by a party
government, supported by a majority party or a coalition of parties and criticized by a minority party or

parties in the lower house. How can it avoid politics and party politics at that? And why should it? A second chamber is part of a political system; its business is politics. It need not be so partisan as a lower house, but it must, unless it is to be completely powerless, express views and take decisions—which usually mean taking sides—on political questions.

3

But if a second chamber is not to be powerless, how much power should it have? The dominant doctrine in Britain and other Commonwealth countries is that a second chamber should be less powerful than the first. There would be a good deal of argument about what its powers should be, but they would be agreed that it would be foolish to make both houses equal in authority. This view would be maintained in Britain, for example, not only because the House of Lords is so composed that, in these days at any rate, it would seem unjustified to allow it to claim equal authority with the Commons. It would be asserted also that it would be foolish to have a second chamber so chosen that it could claim equal authority with the first. For example, if it was decided to elect both houses on universal suffrage from the same constituencies, or from constituencies of different sizes, or if it was decided to elect one house by proportional representation and the other by the single member, simple majority system, there would be produced two houses each representative of the people, and each entitled to claim to speak for the people. Should they not be given equal powers?

The answer would be that this is merely looking for trouble. If the two houses agreed, that would be fortunate, but superfluous. If they disagreed, it would be a nuisance. It would be needlessly adding to the complications and frustrations of government. Indeed if it is desired to have two chambers equally representative and equally powerful, is it not best to do what the Norwegians do—to divide the single chamber after it is elected into two chambers, each representative of the parties in the Storting. Otherwise the only sensible course is to make the second chamber subordinate to the first and so compose it that it ought to be subordinate.

There is, however, a fundamental reason why, in Britain and in many countries of the Commonwealth, it is assumed that second chambers must be subordinate to the first; or, to put it more generally, that, if there are two chambers, one must be subordinate to the other. It arises from their ideas about cabinet government. There is a strong belief in these countries that if there is cabinet government, the cabinet can be responsible to one house only, and that house must be the popularly elected house. If there were two popularly elected houses, unless they were really chosen on identical lines—which seems rather a pointless luxury —complications must immediately arise. Supposing they have different party majorities, it will be impossible to get a cabinet responsible to both. And if you cannot, to which house is the cabinet to be responsible?

This was the sort of problem which the founders of the Australian Constitution had to face at the end of last century when they decided that both the houses of the federal parliament should be popularly elected. They had made things more difficult for themselves by providing that while the House of Representatives should be elected according to population, the second chamber, the Senate, should consist of six (since increased to ten) members from each of the six states, irrespective of population, and what was more, that a half of the Senate should be renewed every three years. So there was plenty of room for a situation where the Senate was of a different party composition from the House. Faced with this dilemma, the Australians were forced to come down on one side and they decided that the Senate should be subordinate to the House of Representatives, and that a cabinet would hold office if and for so long as it had the confidence of the House, whether or not it had a majority in the Senate.

Indeed, it looks at first sight as if wherever there is a system of cabinet government the lower house must be expected to become predominant, whatever the powers given to the second chamber in the Constitution. The Third French Republic used to provide a very good example of this, for in its Constitution it was laid down that ministers were responsible to both houses, yet in practice it was to the lower house, the Chamber of Deputies, that cabinets owed their life and death. Occasionally, it is true, a Prime Minister did resign on defeat in the Senate, but in each case there were strong grounds for believing that he did so because he knew that he had lost the confidence also of the Chamber of Deputies. Yet the French Senate, according to the law of the Constitution, had equal powers with the Chamber. Its consent to Bills was necessary if they were to become law; there was no way of overriding it. None the less the strong tendency in cabinet systems towards the predominance of one chamber prevailed over the letter of the Constitution. It is natural to conclude, therefore, that a cabinet system encourages, if indeed it does not require, the supremacy or at least the superiority of one chamber over the other. A cabinet it would seem must be responsible to one chamber: it cannot be responsible to two.

4

This line of reasoning gains support from the experience of countries where a system of two chambers of equal authority is operated in practice. The United States, in its component states, supplies the greatest number of examples of this system. It abounds in second chambers not only of equal powers with the first, but also elected upon the same franchise, though not usually from the same constituencies. And in the Senate of the United States itself is the great marvel— a second chamber more powerful than the first.

This seems to fit into the pattern exactly. The executive in the United States, both in Washington and in the state capitals, is not responsible to the legislature; it is not necessary to calculate its majority in one house or the other. Its term of office is independent of the party composition of the legislature and it is elected independently. The field is open, therefore, for each of the two houses to make the most of its powers and to assert itself, if it wishes, against the other. Both are elected upon the same franchise, and though upper houses are usually smaller than lower houses and are therefore chosen from larger constituencies, each can claim that in some sense it is representative of the people, or at least that it is just as representative as the other. In the absence, therefore, of any legal differentiation in the powers of the two chambers—save that the Senate of the United States is actually given greater legal powers than the House—and in the absence of a system of cabinet government, it is not surprising to find in the state legislatures of the United States examples of two chambers equal or at any rate comparable in power to each other.

Switzerland gives further evidence of the influence which cabinet government, or the absence of it, can have upon the balance of power between two chambers in a legislature. The Swiss Federal Assembly is bicameral, with a National Council elected proportionately to population and a Council of States equally representative of each of the cantons—much on the lines of the two houses of the American Congress. The Swiss executive, though elected by these two houses in joint session, holds office for a fixed term and is therefore not dependent for its continuance in office upon retaining the confidence of one house or the other. It is true that, since the lower house is larger than the upper, a Swiss executive may be said to owe office in the first place more to the lower house than to the upper, and this may explain why the lower house can be said to have a slight preponderance of power. Yet the difference in authority of the two chambers is not marked. Each in fact has an important say in legislation, and although from time to time one may seem more influential than the other, it is reasonable to conclude that the Swiss, since they lack the cabinet system, have two chambers of equal or comparable power.

5

There is a special reason why the power of the upper houses in the United States and Switzerland is a matter of some concern to their citizens. They are both federal

countries and their constitutions embody the principle
that a mere numerical majority of the population is not
by itself a sufficient authority for taking a decision in
the federal legislature. They believe that their differences are so important that safeguards should be
introduced into the legislative process by which the less
populous parts of the country should be given a
greater authority in the legislature than mere numbers
would justify. So they have the equal representation
of states or cantons in the upper houses to counter-
balance the representation according to population in
the lower. But if this is really to be effective the upper
house must have equal authority with the lower; it
must not be possible for the lower to override the
upper. This balance has been achieved in both these
countries and part of the explanation, it may be suggested, is the fact that they rejected or did not adopt
the cabinet system.

Must it be concluded, then, that in a federation, if it
is desired to safeguard states' rights effectively by a
second chamber, one must not adopt the cabinet
system? This may seem a rather absurd and academic
sort of question. But it is very practical. For if this
conclusion is true it has important consequences for
many countries in the British Commonwealth, for
example, where there has been and still is a fashion
for federalism but where also there is an assumption that
the proper relation between legislature and executive
is the cabinet system, not the presidential or non-
parliamentary executive. All the evidence so far seems
to show that in fact second chambers in federations
in the Commonwealth have not exercised comparable
authority with the lower houses, and that an important,

if not the decisive factor, in bringing this situation about is that they have all adopted the cabinet system. Cabinets, it was recognized from the start, must be responsible to one house only and that house was the lower house, the house elected according to population. In Canada it is not surprising that this result should have occurred, for the Senate there is a body nominated for life and, whatever its legal powers, it was certain that it could not exercise them against a House of Commons elected by the people. In Australia the founders of the Commonwealth saw the issue from the beginning, but even there it would seem that the House of Representatives has predominated over the Senate to a degree which the founders did not intend. This is all the more significant since the Senate is popularly elected upon the same franchise as the House.

It is hard to escape the conclusion that if cabinet government is adopted in a federation, and if it is worked on the assumption accepted in Britain and in Commonwealth countries up to now, a second chamber cannot be an effective safeguard of states' rights, even if it be given in law equal powers with the lower house. The conventions of cabinet government are so strong that, in the end, they will weaken, if not nullify, the legal powers of the second chamber. This is not to say that states' rights cannot be safeguarded in federations where there is a cabinet system; but the safeguards must be provided in other ways.

6

This generalization about the incompatibility of cabinet government and a powerful second chamber, has arisen, let it be remembered, from a discussion based upon the assumptions about the nature and working of cabinet government which are generally held in Britain and the Commonwealth. There are, on the Continent, other ways of doing it as has been seen. It is necessary to say something now about an arrangement in one foreign country which turns upside down all the notions of the possible, or indeed the proper, relations between two chambers which are held in Commonwealth countries. This is the arrangement adopted in Sweden. The Swedes used to have four chambers in their legislature, but they are now content with two. These two are equal in power and the most careful arrangements are made to keep them in line and step. Every Bill introduced goes to a joint committee of the two houses, upon which each house is equally represented, despite their difference in size. Upon report it is considered in both houses simultaneously as far as possible. To avoid the difficulty of requiring ministers to be in two places at once, Bills are arranged on the order paper of the two chambers in such a way that though they are considered at the same sitting, they are not taken in the same order. Then each chamber votes. But what happens if they disagree? The Bill goes back to the joint committee which tries to find an agreeable amendment or solution. But if either chamber refuses to accept the proposed solution, the Bill is dead—with one exception, the budget legislation. If there is disagreement between the two chambers on this matter, the Bill is not referred back to the joint committee. Instead, the chambers vote again and the votes of both chambers are added up and the resultant majority decides the question. This gives a potential predominance to the lower house over the upper because it is larger—230 as against 150—but in practice it has by no means worked out that the lower house has usually won in these differences of opinion. For example, out of ten joint votes held in 1946 and 1947, the upper house won five and the lower won five. That there should be some provision for settling a dispute between the two chambers where a budget Bill is concerned is not surprising. To give the lower house greater weight in deciding a dispute is natural when we remember that its members are directly elected whereas the members of the upper house are indirectly elected, being chosen by provincial councils. As members of the upper house are chosen for eight years, with an eighth retiring each year, it is bound to happen that a fair proportion of them at any time is some distance from contact with the electorate.

Yet, in spite of these marked differences in the method of choosing the two chambers and their terms of office, they are none the less treated as equal and the whole system of government is based upon this principle. The Swedish cabinet is responsible to the two chambers jointly, not to each chamber individually. The Swedes appear to have recognized the tendency under a cabinet system for the cabinet to be responsible only to one chamber and for that chamber to become predominant. They realize that if it is laid down that the cabinet is responsible to both chambers and the matter is left at that, sooner or later one of them, and surely the popularly elected chamber, will become the chamber to which the government is responsible, and thus it will become the predominant house. So they have knitted the two chambers together, and in effect they forbid them to take any important decision separately. Thus there is a real bicameral legislature to which the cabinet is responsible. It might almost be said that, whereas in Norway they have one chamber and pretend to have two, in Sweden they have two and pretend to have one.

There is in this Swedish experience a conception of the relation not only between the two chambers of a legislature, but also between the legislature and the government, which is 'foreign', in more senses than one, to the theory and practice of cabinet government generally accepted in Britain and other Commonwealth countries. It is one more illustration of the system of the stable moderate-to-weak executive, which not merely co-operates and compromises with a lower house, but accepts the control and criticism of an upper house acting jointly with it. But Swedish bicameralism is, like the British House of Lords, unique. And it can be said of it, as of the House of Lords—if it did not exist, you could not invent it.

7

What is the use of a second chamber? Put in the most general terms it seems to be that it provides for a second opinion. Countries differ in the weight which they are prepared to attach to the opinion. In the United States—both in Washington and in the several states—in Sweden, Holland, Belgium, and Italy, for example, no law can be passed without the consent of the upper house. If there is a dispute between the houses, they must agree or the Bill is dead. In some other countries the upper house gives a second opinion, but if the lower house refuses to give way, it can over-ride the opinion of the upper house. This is the position in the United Kingdom, for example, where the House of Commons can pass a money Bill over the opposition of the House of Lords after a maximum delay of one month and can pass any other Bill over the opposition of the House of Lords after a maximum delay of twelve months from the time when the Bill was first given a second reading by the House of Commons —with the significant exception of a Bill to extend the life of parliament, which requires the consent of the House of Lords. In France the Senate has lost the position which it held under the constitution of the Third Republic of being able to veto a Bill absolutely. In the Fourth Republic—where its name was changed to the Council of the Republic—it could hold up a Bill for a maximum of two months, but this delay could be considerably reduced in the case of the budget or of any Bill which the National Assembly had decided to treat as urgent and subject to a time limit. In the Fifth Republic the position of the second chamber—now called the Senate once more—has been strengthened, but even so the government is empowered, after the two houses have failed to agree, to ask the National Assembly to make the final decision. In Ireland, also, it is provided that, if the Senate has not agreed within ninety days to a Bill passed by the Dail, or, in the case of a money Bill, within twenty-one days, the Bills become law.

Moreover, in judging the weight which countries attach to the second opinion of the upper house, it is necessary to look beyond the actual strict letter of the law of the constitution. Although the consent of the upper house of the Netherlands, for example, is necessary for the enactment of a law, that house may not amend Bills; it can only reject them. This weakens its influence. The rule, found in most countries, that financial Bills must originate in the lower house, means that they do not reach the upper house until late in the session, and the pressure upon the upper house to pass them is considerable. What a second chamber may do legally and what it can do in practice is best illustrated perhaps by the Canadian Senate whose consent must be obtained to every Bill. In practice its composition as a nominated house, and the fact that it does not receive most important Bills until late in the session greatly restricts its freedom to influence Bills effectively.

Where a second chamber can do no more than delay a measure, its function becomes that of giving an opportunity for opposition to a Bill to gather its strength or for reconsideration of its terms to be undertaken by the government, and the lower house. In this way some modifications to a Bill may be secured, but even if this does not happen, sufficient time has elapsed in which the attention of the public—so far as it is interested in politics—is directed to the subject matter of the Bill. This can be valuable, though it would be idle to pretend that it is always so.

But are second chambers always so composed that they are capable of giving a valuable second opinion? What have they got that the lower house lacks? Their members have, as a rule, a longer tenure than those of the lower house. They are likely, therefore, to be conservative in the sense of being behind the times. They will reflect the opinions of the electorate over a period of, say, six or eight years, while the lower house reflects the opinion of the electorate of this year or last year or two years before. The upper house then may exercise a brake upon the result of recent electoral success and, who knows, its opinion today may prove to be the opinion of the electorate next year or two years after. An upper house, even if elected on the same franchise and the same constituencies as the lower, can exercise a restraining influence upon it through its longer term and its partial renewal at intervals. And it must be remembered that this 'conservatism' does not mean that it will operate on the side of right-wing interests necessarily. For an upper house may contain a socialist or radical majority as a 'hang over' from previous elections, while the lower house has swung to a conservative or right-wing majority.

Then again it is argued that upper houses, through the longer tenure of their members, have a greater degree of independence towards their party leaders than have the members of lower houses. Moreover in countries where the existence of the cabinet does not depend upon the support of the upper house, its members may speak and vote more freely against the government than can the members of the lower house. Subjects which could not be discussed in the lower house, because the government would frown upon them, can be discussed freely in the upper house. The British House of Lords provides a good example of this position and not least under a Conservative government, when the freedom of Conservative members of the House of Lords to criticize the government and to discuss unpopular subjects is, in fact, at least as great as when a Labour government is in office.

Members of second chambers are regarded, also, as bringing into the legislature the representation of interests and points of view which are likely to be ignored or overwhelmed in the lower house. In particular they are thought to represent rural interests as against urban interests. This is a characteristic often claimed for the senates of the states in the United States, whose electoral districts usually favour the less populous rural areas. Some upper houses in Europe, such as those of Sweden, Belgium, Holland, and France are chosen by local and provincial councils and they reflect in their composition the interests of these areas of the country. When they give their second opinion, therefore, they speak for a part of the country which may be less populous than the urban areas, but is considered socially and economically at least as valuable. This is an argument which is not, of course, accepted by most urban areas or by the parties which derive their strength from them. They are bound to be critical of the powers of upper houses so constituted.

8

Some critics of the way in which upper houses are composed would say that no upper house composed upon the basis of territorial constituencies can offer a second opinion of great value when it considers Bills which have been passed up to it by a lower house which also is based on territorial constituencies. What is needed, they argue, is a second chamber composed on quite different lines and providing a different sort of representation. They have proposed what has been called a vocational second chamber, a functional second chamber or an economic second chamber. Lower houses, they say, represent people in terms of where they live; upper houses should represent them in terms of how they get a living and what they live for. They have been led also to advocate this vocational or functional or economic chamber as a third chamber, either because they have thought it better to avoid the controversy involved in trying to abolish an existing second chamber, or because they have believed that, in some cases at any rate, existing second chambers may perform some useful functions, though they cannot perform those which the functional type of chamber is peculiarly qualified to do.

The Republic of Ireland is thought to provide one of the few examples of a functional second chamber. It was established by the Constitution of 1937 and consists of sixty members. It is composed, apart from eleven members appointed by the Prime Minister, of members elected from five panels of candidates composed of persons having knowledge and practical experience of the national language and culture, literature, art, education, and such other professional interests as may be defined by law; agriculture and allied industries and fisheries; labour, whether organized or unorganized; industry and commerce, including banking, finance, accounting, engineering, and architecture; and public administration and the social services, including voluntary social activities. These candidates submit themselves to election by a college composed of members of the legislature and representatives of local authorities. There are in addition six members elected by the two universities, three by the graduates of the National University of Ireland and three by the graduates of the University of Dublin.

The idea of a functional chamber as a third house found a place in the Constitution of the Fourth French

Republic under the name of the Economic Council, and it was continued, as the Economic and Social Council in the Constitution of the Fifth Republic. Both bodies were composed of persons chosen, in proportions fixed by law, from certain categories of employment or knowledge and they are elected by the principal organizations in those fields. There are representatives of the employees, of industry and commerce, of agriculture, of persons qualified in the economic, social, scientific, or cultural fields, of persons engaged in social service, of producers' co-operatives, of tourism, and of the middle classes. Both bodies were given advisory powers only.

Under the Fourth Republic the government was obliged to submit the national economic plan to the Economic Council. All Bills on economic or social matters, with the exception of the budget, were to be submitted to it before they were debated by the Assembly and its reports on such Bills were to be circulated to the deputies before the debate. Its *rapporteur* had access to the committees of the Assembly and could speak in the debate if the committee or the minister asked him to do so. The Economic Council had the duty also of making a report twice a year on the national income and on means of increasing production, consumption or exports. Moreover, it was given the function of examining and arbitrating in an economic or social conflict at the request of the parties concerned.

The position of the Economic and Social Council under the Fifth Republic appears to be a little stronger. The government may consult it on any social or economic question and it must submit all plans or Bills specifying plans for more than one financial year in the social and economic sphere to it for advice. The Council may designate one of its members to attend and to explain its views before the Senate or the National Assembly. Although it cannot initiate legislation, it may 'call the government's attention' to measures which it thinks would 'encourage the adaptation of economic or social institutions to new techniques'. It was arranged also that the Prime Minister should make an annual report to the Council on the action which the government had taken on its recommendations.

To generalize about the value of functional chambers from the experience of these three institutions would be foolish. But even their short history is instructive. It will be noticed that while the Irish Senate is a part, though clearly a subordinate part of the Irish legislature the Councils of the Fourth and Fifth Republics can hardly be described as integral parts of the French legislature. They are more like a standing advisory conference of experts and interested parties which must or may be consulted but whose consent is not necessary.

This difference of status in relation to the legislature is reflected, it may be suggested, in the way in which in practice the Irish Senate and the French Councils have worked. Though the Irish Senate is on paper a functional or vocational assembly, it has proved in practice to be predominantly a party assembly. By its method of election and by its mode of operation it has consisted almost entirely of members who support one or other of the parties and it always has a government majority. Its nature cannot be better illustrated than by the fact that its members do not sit in vocational groups but are divided, as is the Dail itself, into two sides, with those who support the government sitting on the left of the chairman and those who oppose it sitting on his right. The Irish Senate is, in fact, not an example in practice of a vocational or functional chamber.

The French Councils have in fact worked as vocational chambers. They have debated and reported upon economic and social issues; they have, of course, seldom been unanimous. As a collection of representatives of vested or organized and conflicting interests it would be surprising if they were so. Their task has been to educate the legislature and the government, and also to educate each other. Their influence upon politicians is difficult to judge, but it is enough to say perhaps that their advice can usually be ignored with impunity. It is not surprising that the legislatures of the Fourth and Fifth Republics paid little attention to their views. They provide an example of the value and weakness of vocational chambers.

The fact is that to set up a vocational chamber and give it power, even the power to delay for a few months, raises difficult problems. How is it to be composed? In particular is there to be a majority upon it of employees or of the managerial or employer classes? The answer to this question will probably decide whether the chamber is to have a majority for the left or the right, and this is a matter of great interest to the parties which seek control of the lower house. Inevitably the party in power in the lower house will seek control over the vocational chamber. It seems no accident that the Irish Senate, since it has some power in the legislature, should have become a party chamber. If it had no

function but that of debate and if its consent to legislation was not required, its party composition would be
a matter of less importance. The French Councils
have been able to work as vocational assemblies because
their party political complexion was of negligible concern to the politicians of the National Assembly. The
answer seems inescapable that a functional or vocational chamber can work as such in association with a
party legislature only in an advisory capacity. If it is
intended to be an integral part of the legislature, its
party composition becomes a matter of concern to the
party politicians of the lower house and it will be
converted sooner or later into another party chamber.
Vocational chambers, whether as second or as third
chambers, in societies where politics are conducted on
a free party system, cannot function effectively as an
integral part of the legislature. Their proper sphere lies
outside the legislature.

Chapter Nine

THE DECLINE OF LEGISLATURES?

I

WHEN Lord Bryce was putting together some general conclusions and observations about legislatures in his enormous book *Modern Democracies*, he entitled one chapter 'The Decline of Legislatures'. And he followed it with a chapter called 'The Pathology of Legislatures'. Both chapters really deal with the same question: What are the ills to which legislatures are subject and which cause them to go into decline? A careful study of what Bryce wrote shows that he did not find it possible to give a straight or simple answer to this very general question. It is sometimes assumed, however, by those whose reading may perhaps have gone no further than the chapter headings, that Bryce believed in a general decline of legislatures.

The topic he dealt with many years ago is still of importance today. There are not wanting students of political institutions who speak of the decline of legislatures, of the passing of parliament, of bureaucracy triumphant, and of cabinet or executive dictatorship. Are they right? Is it necessary to apply to legislatures the tribute which that eloquent Congressman, the Hon. Elijah Pogram, paid to the defaulting postmaster in *Martin Chuzzlewit*, and say that their 'bright home is in the setting sun'? It is a very difficult question to answer, but it is necessary to make some attempt at it. If the result is no more than a better understanding of the question itself and of the assumptions upon which it is based, the effort may not have been in vain.

It is helpful in discussing whether or not legislatures have declined to ask in what respect it is asserted that they have or have not declined. Is it a decline in power? Or is it a decline in efficiency? The two do not necessarily go together. A legislature may be doing too much, it may be keeping control of too wide a range of functions and as a result may not have the time or the capacity to perform them effectively. If it declined in power, it might increase in efficiency. Again, is it a decline in public esteem that is alleged? It could be argued with some force that the French legislature did not decline in powers under the Third and Fourth Republics, but none the less it did decline in public esteem. Or it may be that a decline in public interest is suggested. Public esteem and public interest do not necessarily go together. The activities of a legislature may provide a great deal of news: legislators may often be in the public eye; their proceedings may be notorious. But they may stand low in public esteem. Or, finally, in some discussions of the decline of legislatures it would seem that it is a decline in manners, in standards of behaviour which is being asserted.

It is necessary, also, if a sound judgement on the subject is to be reached, to be clear by which standard the alleged decline is being measured. Is it being alleged that legislatures have declined in powers or in efficiency or in public esteem or in public interest in relation to their own former position, or is it that, in relation to other political or social institutions, particularly the executive or party organizations or the

trade unions or employers' organizations or the radio and
television, the decline has occurred. Legislatures may
have retained their own powers or efficiency or prestige
or indeed have increased them, but they may none the
less have declined in these respects relatively to other
institutions which have increased their powers and
improved their position.

If a general survey is made of the position and
working of legislatures in the present century, it is
apparent that, with a few important and striking
exceptions, legislatures have declined in certain important respects and particularly in powers in relation
to the executive government. A feature of the development of political institutions in this period has been
the great growth of executive power as a result largely
of the demands made by two world wars, economic
crises, the adoption of collective or socialist or welfare
policies, and the persistence of international tension.
Governments now do a great deal that they did not do
formerly, but most of what they do was not done by
anybody before. In particular it was not done by the
legislature. The increase of powers by the executive
has not been the result of taking away from the
legislature things which it did before. Legislatures,
indeed, do more than they did and legislators work
longer hours and interest themselves in a wider range
of subjects. Absolutely their powers have increased.
Relatively to the executive government, however, they
have in almost all cases, declined.

In one sphere, perhaps, it looks as if the executive
has taken away a part of the legislature's functions, and
that is in the matter of making the laws. The exercise
by the executive of law-making powers, particularly by

the growth of delegated legislation has meant that the legislature no longer makes all the laws or even all the important laws. Even if we put aside as exceptional and perhaps ephemeral the taking away from the legislature by the executive in France of a large part of the law-making power by the provisions of the Constitution of the Fifth Republic, there remains the fact that in most countries, though the legislature retains the power to make all the laws, it has in fact delegated to the executive the exercise of this power over a wide field. It is true that this delegation can be withdrawn and its exercise controlled, but none the less in practice it is clear that the executive makes part of the laws.

It can be argued, of course, that the legislature itself nowadays spends as much time on law making as ever it did or indeed more time than it did. It deals with important principles, and debates policies which are embodied in statutes. It could not find the time to deal effectively with the mass of rules which are made by the executive under delegated powers. This is true in many countries and to this extent it is permissible to say that the executive is not taking away from the legislature something which it has done or could do. In terms of time devoted to law making and the quantity of its legislative output the legislature may not have declined absolutely; it is only in relation to the executive that it can be said to have declined.

2

Against the background of a decline of legislatures in relation to the executives, there stand out one or two interesting exceptions. In the first place there are examples of legislatures whose position can hardly be said to have declined even relatively as against the executive. One example is the Congress of the United States, whether it be considered as a bicameral legislature or its two chambers be considered separately. It is true that the executive in the United States has increased considerably in its powers in this century, particularly since the inauguration of President Franklin D. Roosevelt. But a strong case can be made for the view that Congress has actually increased its power in the political system and that its position in relation to the executive is at least as strong as it was. There have been times when, as at the beginning of President Franklin Roosevelt's first term, Congress was willing to accept presidential leadership, but quite soon it asserted its independence, and the task of managing Congress has been as complex and difficult since that period as it was before. It may be that the presidency has overshadowed Congress in public interest, and it is natural that the doings of one man should be easier to visualize and to praise or condemn than the complicated workings of groups of representatives and Senators. But congressional committees of inquiry, and individual Senators and Congressmen have rivalled and at times overshadowed the doings of the President. It is, of course, impossible to prove that Congress has or has not declined in relation to the executive. These judgements are matters of impression and opinion. A careful study of the American political system in operation, however, seems to support the judgement that Congress still holds its own with the executive.

A similar judgement may be offered about the position of the French legislature under the Third and

Fourth Republics. Indeed it is possible that some students of French politics might interpret the history of the two Republican constitutions as an illustration of the decline not of the legislature but of the executive. What is certain is that the French legislature maintained its position as the maker and destroyer of cabinets throughout the period, and in this respect it suffered no decline, absolute or relative. Its history raises the question: Is decline necessarily a bad thing? Might it not have been a better thing for France if there had been a decline in the power of the legislature? A stronger cabinet, with some measure of control over the legislature might have improved the efficiency of the legislature itself, in particular in the making of laws. A judgement on this question involves an opinion upon what are the proper functions of a legislature. If one function is to produce and support a government, the French legislature was inefficient, but its inefficiency did not arise from a decline in its power.

In contrast to these two examples of legislatures of which it could be said that they had not suffered a decline as against the executive, it is interesting to look at a group of legislatures which are generally regarded as having declined in this century in power, in public interest and public esteem and in efficiency. These are the legislatures of the states of the United States. There is a passage in the report, published in 1955, of the Commission on Inter-governmental Relations, appointed by President Eisenhower, which summarizes this judgement. 'In the early history of our country', the Report says (p. 38), 'state legislatures were the most powerful and influential instruments of government in the Nation. It was to them that the average citizen looked primarily for initiative and wisdom in the formulation of public policy on domestic issues. They overshadowed the other branches of state government. In power and influence they are no longer as dominant as they were, partly because of the ascendancy of the National Government, partly because of the increased influence of the state executive, but primarily because they have not found effective solutions to problems that become more chronic and more difficult to cope with in a rapidly changing society.' Legislatures of the states or provinces of a federation are in fact likely to have declined in importance because of the growth in power of the central government. The legislatures of the Australian states, of the Canadian provinces or of the Swiss cantons share with the legislatures of the Amercian states this relative decline.

But American state legislatures appear to have suffered a greater loss of power and prestige. A study of the state constitutions suggests that, generally speaking, the citizens of the states apparently do not trust their legislatures, or, at any rate, do not trust them very far. For one thing, they do not seem to feel the need for them. In Britain and in other Commonwealth countries, and in European countries, though citizens may not positively love their legislators, they think they ought to meet at least once a year, and for a fairly substantial period too, so that they may act as a standing committee of grievances, to put it no higher. But only eighteen out of the fifty American states require their legislatures to meet annually; in the others legislatures meet every second year. It is true that in some cases a state governor can call the legislature into extraordinary session, and this power is exercised, but it seems odd that annual sessions are not the usual, ordinary thing.

Then, when the legislatures do meet, they are restricted in what they can do. They are forbidden by the constitutions to pass laws on some matters; on other matters the state constitution itself contains the law in some detail, which the legislature cannot alter. In a number of states the constitution earmarks so high a proportion of the tax revenues that the legislature has the power to deal with less than half of the state's expenditure. In some states the legislatures are not only prevented from making the law on certain matters; when they do exercise law-making powers, they are required to submit the Bill for the approval of the electors at a referendum. And in some states, too, there is a provision for the people themselves to take a hand in the law-making process by the device of the Initiative, by which a certain number of people can put forward a Bill which is submitted for the approval of the electorate. These constitutional limitations are, in the opinion of the Commission on Inter-governmental Relations, an important cause of the ineffectiveness and decline of state legislatures. Restrictions of this kind have, in their opinion, 'engendered at least as many errors and excesses as they have prevented'. It is difficult to resist the conclusion that the state legislatures provide an example of decline in power and prestige in relation both to their own former position and to the position of other political institutions, state and federal.

3

In discussing the relative decline of legislatures it is natural to think first of the effect of the growth in power and importance of the executive. But there are other political and social institutions whose existence and growth have affected the position of the legislature. One important function of a legislature is to be 'a congress of opinions' (in John Stuart Mill's phrase), a forum of debate and discussion on political and social questions. Walter Bagehot in his *English Constitution* described it, in speaking of the British House of Commons, as the 'expressive' function and the 'teaching' function. These functions legislatures have shared with the press for a long period. But the invention of sound radio and television has produced a formidable rival in this sphere. Citizens can now hear and see speakers and debates and discussions on political and social questions which may seem to them to be more interesting and persuasive, less concerned with the arid controversies of party warfare, than what is provided by the speeches of legislators, inside or outside their chambers. The legislature has to take its place as one only and that not always the most impressive of the forums in which public questions are discussed. Public opinion is influenced by these speeches and discussions on the air and legislators find themselves under pressure by their constituents who are less ready to accept the customary explanations. Some legislatures, indeed, have resented the discussion on the radio and television of issues which are being or are about to be discussed by the legislature itself, and have attempted to control this outside discussion. This attitude may be easy to understand, but it is difficult to justify. A wider and freer discussion of public questions may reduce the relative importance of the legislature as a forum of debate, but if it arouses a wider interest in such questions and produces a better informed electorate, it is a good thing.

Some legislatures—Australia and New Zealand are examples—have in fact seized the opportunity provided by radio to broadcast their proceedings or parts of their proceedings. In this way their debates have become better known; a greater number of citizens has an opportunity to hear and to see what goes on in the legislature. Such arrangements could produce an increase in the public interest in the legislature, if not inevitably in the public esteem. There is indeed some dispute about whether legislators behave better or worse when they know that they are being heard or seen by their fellow citizens. It can hardly be doubted that they would behave differently. It is clear, however, that although radio and television may have affected the position of the legislatures as a forum of debate by providing rival forums, they have also provided an instrument by which the work of the legislature may be made known to a far wider public than was ever possible when reliance was placed almost entirely on the press and the public meeting.

There is a further important function of a legislature which it has come to share with other institutions, and that is its function as a committee of grievances, as a body whose members individually and collectively have the task of bringing to the notice of the government and of the public the complaints of the citizens. Here again there is no question of an absolute decline.

The amount of work which legislators do in attending to the complaints or requests of their constituents is greater, not less, than it was fifty years ago. These duties, more perhaps than any others, have converted the post of legislator from a part-time to a full-time job in Britain and in many other countries. At the same time, however, other institutions have taken up some part of the task and do much that would probably remain undone if legislators alone were expected to do it. The great extension of governmental power and services has brought the citizen into contact with the administration to a much greater extent than ever before, and the task of dealing with the complaints and difficulties which arise is more than members of the legislature alone can cope with. This is one reason why the institution of the Ombudsman, as developed in Scandinavia has aroused interest in other countries. New Zealand appointed an Ombudsman in 1962.

Perhaps the principal development which has led to the redress of grievances becoming no longer the exclusive function of the legislature, however, is the growth of trade and professional associations, one of whose chief functions is the promotion and protection of the interests of their members. These organizations cover almost the whole economic and social field, and they are powerful enough and expert enough to be able to take up directly with the administration and at the appropriate level, any complaints or grievances which their members may have. They do not need to work through members of the legislature, though there may be occasions when they find it better to do so. In a wide range of matters, however, it will be more expeditious and more satisfactory both to them and to the executive, if they act direct with the department behind the scenes.

Departments on their side, too, have begun to develop a policy and a technique for dealing with the difficulties and complaints of citizens and to encourage them to come direct to the office with their grievances. The appointment of public relations officers is one example of the methods which the administration uses to deal with complaints and remove misunderstandings. These matters are no longer left exclusively to the minister's explanations in reply to criticisms and questions in the legislature.

4

A discussion of the powers and influence of trade and professional associations and other interest groups leads to a consideration of a further respect in which it is sometimes alleged that legislatures have declined. It is said that they are nowadays much less independent than they were, because so much of importance is decided outside by negotiations between the government and the organized interests concerned, and the task of the legislature is no more than that of applying a rubber stamp. There is certainly some truth in this assertion; what is more difficult to know is the extent of it, whether it has increased, and whether legislatures are, in this respect, roughly where they always were, or have declined in power or independence. It is difficult to avoid the impression that there has been a decline, and that the British House of Commons provides a good example of it. It is also difficult to know what can be done about it. It is not to be expected that the varied interests of a country can be completely and accurately represented in a legislature elected on party lines in territorial constituencies. On the other hand, it would not be thought desirable to have a legislature consisting almost entirely of the representatives of vested interests, however respectable these interests might be. But there must be some machinery through which consultation with interested and affected parties can be carried out and there exists, therefore, in a country like Britain, a whole system of regularly constituted consultative councils and advisory committees whose opinions are available to departments.

There is nothing wrong in this. But the danger is that when things have been worked out very carefully in a department in consultation with these outside bodies, they tend to be presented to the legislature rather as *faits accomplis*. If members criticize them and seek to modify them, they are told, as likely as not, that as these proposals have been worked out carefully, taking into account the views of all those who have been consulted, it is not possible to alter them. It is natural that this should produce a feeling of frustration among legislators, whether on the government or on the opposition side. They feel all the more frustrated, perhaps, because they know that if, at an earlier stage, they had asked for information on the government's intentions and had suggested a debate, they would have been told that, as discussions were still going on, a debate was inadvisable, that no information could be disclosed at this stage, and that negotiations might be put in jeopardy by reason of what might be said in open debate.

In this respect the legislature's function as a forum of debate is affected and not merely its function as a maker

of laws. This is a serious situation. It is indeed
common in the British parliament to hear it said, when
members wish to talk about a subject, that the time is
not ripe. Something is being said or done behind the
scenes which makes it inappropriate to discuss the
matter in public just now. In international affairs it is
often possible to see the force of this argument, but not
perhaps quite so often as it is put forward. In home
affairs it is usually harder to accept. There is indeed a
difficult dilemma here. On the one hand there is the
situation where legislators talk too soon—and the
United States Congress has provided examples of this;
on the other there is the situation of which the British
House of Commons is an example, where, when a
member may talk, he may talk too late.

5

Much of the discussion of the decline of legislatures
is based on the assumption that decline was possible.
There is a myth of a golden age of legislatures when
wisdom and oratory and gentlemanly behaviour and
public spirit all seemed somehow to flourish and to
flourish together. It is difficult to know when this could
have been. Bryce himself believed that in some countries there had been no decline, for the standard had
not been high enough to admit of the possibility of
decline. His choice of examples—Australia and
Canada—cannot have pleased everybody; some might
have expected him to find examples more readily in
Central and South America.

Evidence for the existence of the golden age is not
easy to weigh. There were great orators in the British
House of Commons in the nineteenth century, but the

voice of Churchill in the twentieth was as great as the voice of Gladstone in the nineteenth. And is oratory to be preferred to a simple conversational style? Were the speeches of members of parliament in the nineteenth century more interesting to their hearers than those in the twentieth century? Were there not bores who specialized in economics and foreign relations in those days as in these? If we are to speak of a decline in manners, it is proper to remark that there has never occurred in the House of Commons since 1919 disorder of the kind or degree which was a feature of the eighteen-eighties when the Irish members were at their liveliest, or in the years between 1909 and 1914 when Lloyd George's budget, the reform of the House of Lords, and Irish Home Rule were under discussion. It is not too much to assert that the House of Commons is better behaved since 1919 than in the century before that date. It is hard to escape the conclusion that the golden age recedes as we approach it.

The fact is that the decline of legislatures may be an interesting question to discuss in general terms, but it is difficult if not impossible to decide. If we try to make the question more precise, we may confine ourselves to a discussion of decline in efficiency. We must then ask ourselves: What are legislatures for? What functions ought they to perform? The answer will not be the same in all cases. For one thing, the question of size intrudes itself once more. There are some things a legislature of 100 members or less can do which a legislature of 600 or more cannot do. But one or two assertions of general validity can be made. It is not the function of a legislature to be the sole forum of debate or the sole committee of grievances in its country's political system; these functions must and should be shared with other bodies. It is not the function of a legislature to govern. These are truisms, yet it is the unwillingness of legislatures to give up the claim and the attempt to be and to do all these things that has resulted, in many countries, in a decline not in powers but in efficiency. To do less and, perhaps thereby, to do it better, may often prove to be the best safeguard against the decline of legislatures.

SELECT BIBLIOGRAPHY

I. A bare minimum of information about the legislatures of all countries is provided in the annual volumes of *The Political Handbook of the World* (New York: Harper and Bros. for the Council on Foreign Relations). Two books issued by the Inter-Parliamentary Union make a comparative study of a number of legislatures. They are Lord Campion and D. W. S. Lidderdale, *European Parliamentary Procedure* (London: Allen and Unwin, 1953) and *Parliaments* (London: Cassell, 1962), the latter dealing with forty-one countries, including Albania and Monaco but excluding Canada and New Zealand. Among journals may be mentioned *Parliamentary Affairs*, published quarterly by the Hansard Society, which is full of interesting and informative articles; *The Table*, the annual publication of the Society of Clerks-at-the-Table, which is concerned with legislatures of the Commonwealth; the *Journal of the Parliaments of the Commonwealth*; *Public Law*; and *The American Political Science Review*.

II. Books on the legislatures of particular countries are numerous and it is not always easy to select. American state and federal legislatures are dealt with comparatively in Harvey Walker, *The Legislative Process* (New York: The Ronald Press Co., 1948). Much information about the state legislatures is provided in *The Book of the States* published every two years by the Council of State Governments. Among books on Congress may be mentioned George B. Galloway, *The Legislative Process in Congress* (New York: Crowell Co., 1953); Ernest S. Griffith, *Congress: Its Contemporary Role* (New York: New York University Press, rev. ed., 1956), and, with emphasis on procedure, Floyd M. Riddick, *The*

United States Congress: Its Organisation and Procedure
(National Capitol Publishers, Inc., Manassas, Virginia,
1949).

Sir Ivor Jennings, *Parliament* (Cambridge University
Press, 3rd ed., 1960), is the standard book on the British
legislature. The reader will find much of interest also in
Roland Young, *The British Parliament* (London: Faber
and Faber, 1962), Eric Taylor, *The House of Commons at
Work* (London: Penguin Books, 3rd ed., 1958), Sir C.
Ilbert and Sir C. Carr, *Parliament* (London: Oxford
University Press, 3rd ed., 1948), S. Gordon, *Our
Parliament* (London: Hansard Society, 4th ed., 1958),
Herbert Morrison, *Government and Parliament* (Oxford
University Press, 2nd ed., 1959), H. J. Laski, *Parlia-
mentary Government in England* (London: Allen and
Unwin, 1938). The authoritative work on procedure is
Sir T. Erskine May, *The Law, Privileges, Proceedings
and Usage of Parliament* (London: Butterworth and Co.,
16th ed., 1957) referred to with respect in all the legisla-
tures of the Commonwealth.

Books in English on the French legislature are rare.
D. W. S. Lidderdale, *The Parliament of France* (London:
Hansard Society, 1951) gives a full account of the procedure of the legislature of the Fourth Republic, but is
rather technical in its approach. A discussion of the
French legislature, in its place as part of the political
system, is found in such books as W. R. Sharp, *The Government of the French Republic* (New York: Van Nostrand,
1939) for the Third Republic, Philip Williams, *Politics in
Post-War France* (London: Longmans, 1954) for the
Fourth, and Philip Williams and Martin Harrison, *De
Gaulle's Republic* (London: Longmans, 2nd ed., 1961)
for the Fifth.

Among books on the legislatures of other countries
may be mentioned four published by the Hansard Society
—Elis Hastad, *The Parliament of Sweden* (1957), C. J.

Hughes, *The Parliament of Switzerland* (1962), E. Van Raalte, *The Parliament of the Kingdom of the Netherlands* (1959), and S. King-Hall and R. K. Ullmann, *German Parliaments* (1956). Some useful discussion of the legislatures of the countries concerned is to be found in such books as S. R. Davis (ed.) *The Government of the Australian States* (London: Longmans, 1956), A. F. Davies, *Australian Democracy* (London: Longmans, 1958), J. D. B. Miller, *Australian Government and Politics* (London: Duckworth, 2nd ed., 1959), L. F. Crisp, *Parliamentary Government of the Commonwealth of Australia* (London: Longmans, 1949), W. H. Morris Jones, *Parliament in India* (London: Longmans, 1957), A. R. Mukharjea, *Parliamentary Procedure in India* (Oxford University Press, 1958), Alexander Brady, *Democracy in the Dominions* (University of Toronto Press, 2nd ed., 1952), B. A. Arneson, *The Democratic Monarchies of Scandinavia* (New York: Van Nostrand, 2nd ed., 1949), Dankwart A. Rustow, *The Politics of Compromise* (Princeton University Press, 1955), a study of Swedish parliamentary institutions, R. Mc.G. Dawson, *The Government of Canada* (Toronto University Press, 3rd ed., revised, 1960), and R. Hiscocks, *Democracy in Western Germany* (Oxford University Press, 1957).

III. On electoral systems the best short book is W. J. M. Mackenzie, *Free Elections* (London: Allen and Unwin, 1958). The case for proportional representation is supported in Enid Lakeman and J. D. Lambert *Voting in Democracies* (London: Faber and Faber, 1955). J. F. S. Ross, *Elections and Electors* (London: Eyre and Spottiswoode, 1955) and *Parliamentary Representation* (same publishers, rev. ed., 1956) are interesting and valuable for the British system. The bewildering changes in the electoral laws of France are most lucidly explained in Peter Campbell, *French Electoral Systems and Elections, 1789–1957* (London: Allen and Unwin, 1958).

Of the increasing number of studies of actual elections, there may be mentioned the series on British General Elections sponsored by Nuffield College, Oxford—R. B. McCallum and A. Readman, *The British General Election of 1945* (Oxford University Press, 1947), H. G. Nicholas, *The British General Election of 1950* (Macmillan, 1951), D. E. Butler, *The British General Election of 1951* (Macmillan, 1952), *The British General Election of 1955* (Macmillan, 1955) and D. E. Butler and R. Rose, *The British General Election of 1959* (Macmillan, 1960). Reference may be made also to W. J. M. Mackenzie and K. E. Robinson (eds.) *Five Elections in Africa* (Oxford: at the Clarendon Press, 1960), T. E. Smith, *Elections in Developing Countries* (London: Macmillan, 1960), U. Kitzinger, *German Electoral Politics* (Oxford: at the Clarendon Press, 1960) and D. E. Butler (ed.) *Elections Abroad* (London: Macmillan, 1959).

IV. The influence of pressure groups upon legislatures is studied in J. D. Stewart, *British Pressure Groups* (Oxford: at the Clarendon Press, 1958), H. W. Ehrmann (ed.) *Interest Groups in Four Continents* (University of Pittsburgh Press, 1958), which deals with Australia, Finland, France, Germany, Great Britain, Japan, Sweden, the United States, and Jugoslavia; and for the United States, V. O. Key, *Politics, Parties and Pressure Groups* (New York: Crowell Co., 4th ed., 1958).

V. Among studies of particular aspects of the British legislature may be mentioned the following: D. N. Chester and N. Bowring, *Questions in Parliament* (Oxford: at the Clarendon Press, 1962), P. A. Bromhead, *Private Members Bills in the British Parliament* (1956), and *The House of Lords and Contemporary Politics* (1958), both published by Routledge and Kegan Paul, London; Nigel Nicolson, *People and Parliament* (London: Weidenfeld and Nicolson, 1958), an account of the relations between an M.P. and his constituents; and P. G.

Richards, *Honourable Members*, a study of British back-benchers (Faber, 1959).

VI. All who wish to understand legislatures should avoid the error of being merely up-to-date. A study of the out-of-date classics and of books which trace the history of legislatures is indispensable. For this purpose reference may be made to J. S. Mill, *Representative Government* (1861), Walter Bagehot, *The English Constitution* (1867), Woodrow Wilson, *Congressional Government* (1885), A. Lawrence Lowell, *The Government of England* (2 vols., 1908), and *Governments and Parties in Continental Europe* (2 vols., 1896), James Bryce, *The American Commonwealth* (3 vols., 1888), Joseph Redlich, *The Procedure of the House of Commons* (3 vols., 1907).

INDEX